# CAREER CHOICES
## *for Students of*
❂
# POLITICAL SCIENCE AND GOVERNMENT

*by*
## CAREER ASSOCIATES

❀

*Walker and Company*
NEW YORK

Copyright © 1985 by Walker and Company, Inc.

First published in the United States of America in 1985 by the Walker Publishing Company, Inc.

Published simultaneously in Canada by John Wiley & Sons Canada, Limited, Rexdale, Ontario.

**Library of Congress Cataloging in Publication Data**
Main entry under title:

Career choices for students of political science and government.

Bibliography: p.
1. United States—Occupations. 2. College graduates—Employment—United States. 3. Vocational guidance—United States. I. Career Associates.
HF5382.5.U5C25557 1985     331.7′023     83-40442
ISBN 0-8027-0797-1
ISBN 0-8027-7247-1 (pbk.)

Printed in the United States of America

10 9 8 7 6 5 4 3 2 1

# Titles in the Series

Career Choices For Students Of:

Art
Business
Communications and Journalism
Computer Science
Economics
English
History
Mathematics
Political Science and Government
Psychology

Career Choices For Undergraduates Considering:

Law
An M.B.A.

# Acknowledgments

We gratefully acknowledge the help of the many people who spent time talking to our research staff about employment opportunities in their fields. This book would not have been possible without their assistance. Our thanks, too, to Catalyst, which has one of the best career libraries in the country in its New York, NY offices, and to the National Society for Internships and Experiential Education, Raleigh, NC, which provided information on internship opportunities for a variety of professions.

The chapter on legal careers came about only through the excellent efforts of Lynn Stephens Strudler, Assistant Dean of the New York University School of Law Placement Office; special thanks, also, to the staff of researchers and interviewers who took time from their duties as law placement officers to gather the information in this chapter. Kayle Tucker of the National Newspaper Association was particularly generous with her time and evaluation of information contained in this book.

# CAREER ASSOCIATES

| | |
|---|---|
| Senior Editor-Series Development: | Peggy J. Schmidt |
| Project Editor: | M. J. Territo |
| Series Editorial Assistant | Alan Selsor |
| Editors: | Ruth Cavin |
| | Jill Gorham |
| | Andrea Fooner |
| | Linda Peterson |
| Researchers-Writers: | Norma P. D'Apolito |
| | Pam Diamond |
| | Adrienne Diehr |
| | Roxanne Farmanfarmaian |
| | Carol Kanarek |
| | Gail Kislevitz |
| | Barbara Milton |
| | Marilyn Norton |
| | Alan Selsor |
| | Lynn Stephens Strudler |
| Researchers: | Fletcher Harper |
| | Deirdre Swords |
| | Martha Sutro |
| | Ernest Tracey, III |
| | Ramsey Walker |

Series Concept Created by Ramsey Walker

# CONTENTS

# WHAT'S IN THIS BOOK FOR YOU?

Recent college graduates, no matter what their major has been, too often discover that there is a dismaying gap between their knowledge and planning and the reality of an actual career. Possibly even more unfortunate is the existence of potentially satisfying careers that graduates do not even know about. Although advice from campus vocational counselors, family, friends, and fellow students can be extremely helpful, there is no substitute for a structured exploration of the various alternatives open to graduates.

The Career Choices Series was created to provide you with the means to conduct such an exploration. It gives you specific, up-to-date information about the entry-level job opportunities in a variety of industries relevant to your degree and highlights opportunities that might otherwise be overlooked. Through its many special features—such as sections on internships, qualifications, and working conditions—the Career Choices Series can help you find out where your interests and abilities lie in order to point your search for an entry-level job in a productive direction. This book cannot find you a job—only you can provide the hard work, persistence, and ingenuity that that requires—but it can save you valuable time and energy. By helping you to narrow the range of your search to careers that are truly suitable for you, this book can help make hunting for a job an exciting adventure rather than a dreary—and sometimes frightening—chore.

The book's easy-to-use format combines general information about each of the industries covered with the hard facts that job-hunters must have. An overall explanation of each industry is followed by authoritative material on the job outlook for entry-level candidates, the competition for the openings that exist, and the new opportunities that may arise from such factors as expansion and technological development. There is a listing of employers by type and by geographic location and a sampling of leading companies by name—by no means all, but enough to give you a good idea of who the employers are.

The section on how to break into the field is not general how-to-get-a-job advice, but rather zeroes in on ways of getting a foot in the door of a particular industry.

You will find the next section, a description of the major functional areas within each industry, especially valuable in making your initial job choice. For example, communications majors aiming for magazine work can evaluate the editorial end, advertising space sales, circulation, or production. Those interested in accounting are shown the differences between management, government, and public accounting. Which of the various areas described offers you the best chance of an entry-level job? What career paths are likely to follow from that position? Will they help you reach your ultimate career goal? The sooner you have a basis to make the decision, the better prepared you can be.

For every industry treated and for the major functional areas within that industry, you'll learn what your duties—both basic and more challenging—are likely to be, what hours you'll work, what your work environment will be, and what salary to expect.*What personal and professional qualifications must you have? How can you move up—and to what? This book tells you.

You'll learn how it is possible to overcome the apparent contradiction of the truism, "To get experience you have to have experience." The kinds of extracurricular activities and work experience—summer and/or part-time—that can help you get and perform a job in your chosen area are listed. Internships are another way to get over that hurdle, and specific information is included for each industry. But you should also know that the directories published by the National Society for Internships and Experiential Education (Second Floor, 124 St. Mary's Street, Raleigh, NC 27605) are highly detailed and very useful. They are: *Directory of Undergraduate Internships, Directory of Washington Internships,* and *Directory of Public Service Internships.*

You'll find a list of the books and periodicals you should read to keep up with the latest trends in an industry you are considering, and the names and addresses of professional associations that can be helpful to you—through student chapters, open meetings, and printed information. Finally, interviews with professionals in each

---

* Salary figures given are the latest available as the book goes to press.

field bring you the experiences of people who are actually working in the kinds of jobs you may be aiming for.

Although your entry-level job neither guarantees nor locks you into a lifelong career path, the more you know about what is open to you, the better chance you'll have for a rewarding work future. The information in these pages will not only give you a realistic basis for a good start, it will help you immeasurably in deciding what to explore further on your own. So good reading, good hunting, good luck, and the best of good beginnings.

---

\*

---

# BANKING

IMAGINE yourself the manager of an operations department, responsible for the global transfer of currencies worth several million dollars. Or a member of the international department, traveling to the Middle East, Africa, or Europe to check on overseas branches. Or managing a loan portfolio for a major multinational corporation, providing its chief financial officer with up-to-date financial information. Banking has become the central nervous system of the world's economy, and today's dynamic banker can be found in front of a desk-top terminal calling up the vast amount of financial data needed to provide an increasing array of new products and services. Today customers want banks to provide more than brokerage services and electronic funds transfers. If you want to be involved in a state-of-the-art business, if you have an entrepreneurial spirit, and, above all, if you are endowed with keen creativity, a career in banking is for you.

The changes in banking are primarily due to the impact of technology. Banking is now a worldwide, 24-hour-a-day business. Automated teller machines, home banking via microcomputers, and office automation have affected every bank employee. But you don't have to be a whiz kid who talks in bits and bytes to get your foot in the door. Every major bank has either a formal training program or professional on-the-job training that includes instruction in the use of the technology. What is most important is your ability to grasp the concept and quickly master the skill.

Banks recruit graduates from a wide variety of majors. In fact, half of all college students entering banking come from a liberal arts background. But don't overlook the traditional financial core courses: business, accounting, marketing, and finance. They will add to your desirability as a job candidate, as will a knowledge of computer science, production management (operations), and interpersonal communications. When a recruiter is having a hard time deciding, it is your interpersonal skills that will count most heavily.

Most banks put their college recruits through a formal training program in which they are taught the methods and practices of the particular institution. Regardless of academic background, all newcomers go into the same melting pot. Students who have taken the financial core courses mentioned will, of course, be more familiar with those subjects during the training program. However, strong analytical skills will enable you to interpret a financial statement, and here an English major who knows how to extract meaning from a careful reading of literature or a history major who knows how to spot a trend or movement in a group of facts will not be at a disadvantage to a finance major.

More and more students entering the field have had the foresight to make themselves knowledgeable about telecommunications to gain an understanding of the newly diverse world of banking. These students have a better chance of getting a job offer than those with a limited, traditional view of the industry.

Many different functional areas exist within banking, and most banks will ask you for which area you prefer to be considered. Commercial and retail banking have recruitment programs in the following functional areas:

- **Credit Lending**
- **Operations**

- **Systems**
- **Trusts**

## Job Outlook

*Job Openings Will Grow:* Faster than average

*Competition for Jobs:* Keen
Expect the most competition for positions in credit lending. Expanding opportunities can be found in the operations and systems areas. As new sources for loans become harder to find, operations is being looked to for development of nonfee-based services, such as letters of credit and money transfer services. In systems, the computerization and communications systems needed to deliver customer services are implemented.

*New Job Opportunities:* Because of industry deregulation, banks are now actively seeking people to work in such diverse areas as mergers and acquisitions; private banking, which serves individuals with high net worth and high incomes; office automation, which develops executive information systems and implements them throughout the bank; product management, which includes the planning, pricing, and marketing of new products and services; and telecommunications, which develops the global communications channels necessary for getting and submitting information.

## Geographic Job Index

Although banks can be found in any city or town, the major money centers are located in New York, NY, Chicago, IL, San Francisco, CA and Boston, MA. Opportunities at the regional or local end of the industry are growing in Dallas, TX, Houston, TX, and other cities in the Southwest.

## Who the Employers Are

COMMERCIAL BANKS (or money-center banks) market their products and services to multinational corporations; to smaller banks, called correspondents; and to individuals, who use checking and loan services.

**REGIONAL BANKS** provide many of the same services as the larger money-center banks, but on a smaller scale. Their clients are typically locally based small and medium-size businesses.

**SAVINGS AND LOAN ASSOCIATIONS** offer their customers personal savings accounts and mortgages. However, under new banking legislation, they are allowed to make commercial and business loans.

## Major Employers

**COMMERCIAL BANKS**
> Bank of America, San Francisco, CA
> Bankers Trust Company, New York, NY
> Chase Manhattan Bank, New York, NY
> Chemical Bank, New York, NY
> Citibank, New York, NY
> Continental Illinois National Bank, Chicago, IL
> First National Bank of Boston, Boston, MA
> First National Bank of Chicago, Chicago, IL
> Manufacturers Hanover Trust Company, New York, NY
> Security Pacific National Bank, Los Angeles, CA

**REGIONAL BANKS**
> First Bank System, Minneapolis, MN
> Mellon Bank, Pittsburgh, PA
> Mercantile Bank, St. Louis, MO
> NCNB National Bank, Charlotte, NC
> Ranier National Bank, Seattle, WA
> Republic Bank Dallas, Dallas, TX
> Wachovia Bank & Trust Company, Winston-Salem, NC

### How to Break into the Field

Most banks have formal on-campus recruitment programs through which they hire most of their trainees. They frequently recruit separately for each major functional area: credit lending, operations, systems, and trusts. Be sure to check schedules carefully to ensure an appointment in your area of interest.

Before the interview, do your homework. Learn all you can about the internal workings of the area for which you plan to interview. If your field of interest is not represented, select the next most appropriate area and ask the recruiter to forward your résumé to the proper section. Also, learn something about the bank itself. Different banks have different personalities. Some are aggressive, others more traditional and conservative. Try to interview with banks that have a corporate identity compatible with your own personal identity.

Landing a summer internship is another pathway to a full-time position. Most major banks have internship programs, although they are usually limited to graduate students. Recruitment for the internships is usually done through campus visits. Check with your placement office for details.

If your college does not have a formal placement office, or if the bank to which you wish to apply is not recruiting on your campus, send a well-written letter, accompanied by a résumé, to the bank's director of college recruitment. Follow up your letter with a phone call.

Whether you have an on-campus interview or are writing directly to the college recruitment department, never pass up help from anyone who knows someone at the bank. A well-placed word can be invaluable.

## International Job Opportunities

At a large commercial bank, and even at some regional banks, overseas work is possible. International department lending officers may be assigned to work abroad for a period of three to five years, or may be required to travel abroad frequently. Corporate department staffs that handle U.S. multinational corporations also do quite a bit of business overseas.

Most banks try to staff their overseas branches with local citizens. Only the higher-level managerial jobs may be filled by Americans. Specialized positions in areas such as investment banking, joint ventures, and trade go to M.B.A.s or other experienced personnel. Fluency in a foreign language is helpful but not essential, because most banks have contracts with language schools to provide training as necessary.

# CREDIT LENDING

This is the most visible area of banking, the area that involves the traditional bank-client relationship that almost everyone associates with the industry. However, this aspect of banking is more than just extending credit or offering interest-bearing accounts to clients. In consumer banking, a lending officer assesses the creditworthiness of individuals. In commercial banking, a lending officer evaluates the financial status of corporations or nonprofit organizations; performs industry surveys, analyzing a particular industry to determine if backing a firm in that area is a good loan risk; makes production forecasts to see if a borrowing firm's available resources will meet production requirements; predicts how a loan would affect the bank's cash flow positively or negatively; or handles corporate overdrafts, contacting corporate customers whose payments are late.

To start out you will go on customer calls with experienced loan officers and be responsible for taking notes and writing a report on the customer and the loan review—not as a participant, but as an observer. You may be called on to research new business prospects, making cold calls to prospects in a given territory or industry. At a smaller bank, your responsibilities will be broader and you will actually make decisions on modest loans quite early.

## Qualifications

*Personal:*  Strong analytical skills. Ability to conceptualize. An affinity for quantitative problems. Strong negotiation skills. Extremely good interpersonal skills.

*Professional:* Ability to analyze data and financial statements and do creative financial planning. Familiarity with bank products and services. Ability to present clearly written reports.

## Career Paths

| LEVEL | JOB TITLE | EXPERIENCE NEEDED |
|-------|-----------|-------------------|
| Entry | Trainee | College degree |
| 2 | Assistant Loan Officer | 1-2 years |
| 3 | Loan Officer/Branch manager | 3-5 years |
| 4 | Loan manager | 7+ years |

## Job Responsibilities

### Entry Level

THE BASICS: Training will consist of both classroom instruction in such areas as finance, accounting, and credit analysis, and actual account work, helping lending officers make judgments about existing or potential bank relationships.

MORE CHALLENGING DUTIES: Upon completion of training, you will be assigned to a line lending area, attend advanced banking seminars, and have the opportunity to meet with customers.

### Moving Up

Your advancement will depend on your ability to establish advantageous client relationships, to close lucrative loan deals successfully, and to know when not to approve a loan. As you advance, the loan review process will become more complex and involve significantly more money. You can measure your success by your approval authority—how big a loan you are authorized to approve without going to a higher level of management.

# OPERATIONS

The most successful banks anticipate and satisfy all their customers' financial needs. Operations occupies a front-row seat in the banking industry because it has bankwide responsibility for providing customers with nonfee-based (nonloan) services—letters of credit, money transfers, and foreign exchange—services of increased importance because banks can no longer make the profits they once did by lending money to customers. The operations department is usually the largest department of a commercial bank. The Chase Manhattan Bank operations department, for example, has more than 4,000 employees. Graduates are employed in supervisory positions, managing the clerical staff, with responsibility for setting up assignments and time schedules, evaluating performance, making sure work is done properly, training new employees, and authorizing salary increases. Work in operations also involves troubleshooting for customers, solving their account problems, for example, by tracing a money transfer that was never credited.

## Qualifications

*Personal:*   Ability to meet deadlines. Ability to perform under pressure. Ability to get along with many different types of people.

*Professional:*   Ability to understand and follow through on complex instructions. Familiarity with concepts of computer science or a related discipline. Knowledge of fee-based services and products.

## Career Paths

| LEVEL | JOB TITLE | EXPERIENCE NEEDED |
|-------|-----------|-------------------|
| Entry | Operations Trainee | College degree |
| 2 | Supervisor | 18 months |
| 3 | Department manager | 3-5 years |
| 4 | Division manager | 6+ years |

## Job Responsibilities

### Entry Level

**THE BASICS:**   You begin your career in operations either in a formal training program, or, more likely, on the job. You will be an operations trainee for about 18 months, learning by rotating among the various departments that handle fee-based services.

**MORE CHALLENGING DUTIES:**   After the training period, you will be assigned to a department or a staff area such as financial management or budget coordination and will learn about a single product or area in depth.

### Moving Up

Your progress will depend on your ability to improve the overall productivity of your department or area, to motivate your staff, to stay within your budget, and to complete transactions efficiently and accurately. Because operations is not exclusively devoted to production management, for further advancement you will need to learn about product development, marketing, and systems functions. Those who move into these areas often accompany loan officers on customer calls, offering the technical advice that will help clinch a deal or presenting a plan to customize an existing product to meet the client's expanding needs.

With hard work and diligence you can acquire the knowledge and expertise that will enable you to move almost anywhere in the bank organization. Operations managers can move into marketing positions, the systems areas, or perhaps relocate (even overseas) to manage a branch bank.

# SYSTEMS

The systems area is now involved in every banking decision from credit lending to recruitment. Most large commercial banks have both a central systems area and separate decentralized systems units that service the major components of the organization. Systems is responsible for developing, implementing, and maintaining automated programs for clients and for in-house use; for selecting hardware, writing software, and consulting with the user-client when special programs must be developed. In addition, systems staffers must keep up with the latest developments in technological applications and services.

## Qualifications

*Personal:*   Ability to think in analytical terms. Ease in working with abstract models.

*Professional:*   Quantitative skills. Familiarity with the business applications of software and hardware. Ability to convert technical language and concepts into familiar and understandable terms.

## Career Paths

| LEVEL | JOB TITLE | EXPERIENCE NEEDED |
|---|---|---|
| Entry | Systems trainee | College degree |
| 2 | Systems analyst | 2 years |
| 3 | Systems consultant | 3 years |
| 4 | Senior systems consultant | 5 years |

## Job Responsibilities

### Entry Level

**THE BASICS:** Either in a structured training program or through on-the-job-training, you will become familiar with the bank's hardware and software and how they are used. Depending on your background, you may become a programmer, or you may be placed on a systems team project, refining the use of current equipment or developing systems for as yet unmet needs.

**MORE CHALLENGING DUTIES:** Applying your skills to more difficult or specialized projects.

### Moving Up

If you demonstrate interpersonal skills as well as technical ability, you could become a project manager, overseeing a team of systems people working on the development and implementation of a specific systems capability, such as a new internal telephone switching system or software for an executive work station, which could include features such as electronic mail and word processing.

The potential for a talented systems person is excellent. You could end up managing an operations or office automation department, developing and installing new systems, or becoming a systems consultant for overseas branches. Successful systems personnel can move into any department in the bank.

# TRUSTS

The trust department manages and invests money, property, or other assets owned by a client. The pension plans of large corporations and other organizations often use trusts, as do individuals with large assets. Many estates are also managed in trust by the provisions of a will. Like the credit department, this department deals closely and extensively with clients. The training program is similar to that in other areas of banking, but in general advancement is slower and requires more experience.

## Qualifications

*Personal:*   A straightforward manner. Accuracy. Good with numbers. Patience in dealing with people. Confidence.

*Professional:*   Strong analytical ability. Good business judgment. Ability to apply financial theory to practical problems.

## Career Paths

| LEVEL | JOB TITLE | EXPERIENCE NEEDED |
|-------|-----------|-------------------|
| Entry | Trainee | College degree |
| 2 | Assistant trust officer | 1-3 years |
| 3 | Trust officer | 4-6 years |
| 4 | Senior trust officer | 10+ years |

## Job Responsibilities

### Entry Level

**THE BASICS:** Developing familiarity with bank policies and procedures.

**MORE CHALLENGING POSITIONS:** Researching investments, real estate, or the overall economy to assist superiors. Some contact with clients.

### Moving Up

Showing sound judgment and an ability to work independently will garner an assignment to manage some of the smaller trust funds. Moving up also depends on your ability to attract new customers to the bank, as well as to keep present clients satisfied. As you advance you will become responsible for handling more and more money. Top-level trust officers are expected not only to bring in substantial new business and to handle the largest accounts, but also to manage and support lower-level employees.

## ADDITIONAL INFORMATION

### Salaries

Salaries vary according to the size of the bank. The following figures are taken from Robert Half International's 1984 survey:

Installment loans/assistant manager: $18,000 to $22,000 (small bank); $21,000 to $27,000 (medium-size bank); $23,500 to $28,500 (large bank).

Commercial loans/branch manager: $22,000 to $28,000 (small); $24,000 to $31,000 (medium); $26,000 to $31,000 (large).

Senior loan officer:   $28,000 to $32,000 (small); $33,000 to $37,000 (medium); $33,000 to $50,000 (large).

Mortgage loans:   $23,500 to $32,000 (small); $28,000 to $36,000 (medium); $32,000 to $41,000 (large).

Operations officer:   $17,000 to $21,000 (small); $22,000 to $29,000 (medium); $24,000 to $31,000 (large).

Trust officer:   $22,000 to $29,500 (small); $23,000 to $30,000 (medium); $27,500 to $40,000 (large).

## Working Conditions

*Hours:*   The credit trainee rarely sees daylight, because long hours and weekend work are often required to get through the training program. After training, normal hours will be whatever it takes to get the job done (nine to five plus). The hours in operations are different because it is a 24-hour-a-day shop. Night shifts and weekend work may be unavoidable, especially for less experienced employees. Systems staffers may also work on a 24-hour clock; the hours are longest when new systems are being installed and deadlines must be met.

*Environment:*   Lending officers get the choicest locations in the bank; because their job is customer-oriented, the surroundings are usually plush and pleasant. The operations and systems departments take a 360-degree turn from the lending department; the workspace is strictly functional, with few amenities.

*Workstyle:*   In credit, much time is spent researching facts and figures about existing and prospective clients, which could take you from the bank library to the client's headquarters. The rest of your time will largely be spent in conference with senior lending officers. Operations and systems work is desk work. Managers walk the area, talking with the staff and lending assistance. In both departments, senior people may meet occasionally with systems consultants.

*Travel:* Travel is rare for entry-level employees in any bank. Later, however, lending officers in consumer banking might travel throughout their state. In commercial banking, research could take a lending officer to major cities throughout the country. If you are assigned to the international department in credit, operations, or systems, you might be sent to overseas branches.

## Extracurricular Activities/Work Experience

Experience as a cashier/teller

Clerical experience

Financial officer/treasurer in campus organizations

## Internships

Many banks—savings and loan associations and consumer and commercial banks—are willing to take interns, especially in summer programs. Interns are paid, and the experience may result in a job offer after graduation. Your campus placement office is the best source of information regarding these programs. If your school does not have a placement office, contact the college recruitment director at banks that interest you for details.

## Recommended Reading

**BOOKS**

*All You Need to Know About Banks* by John Cook and Robert Wood, Bantam Books: 1983

*The Bankers* by Martin Mayer, Ballantine Books: 1980

*In Banks We Trust* by Penny Lernoux, Doubleday & Company: 1984

*Money: Bank of the Eighties* by Dimitris Chorafas, Petrocelli: 1981

*Money and Banking* by Richard W. Lindholm, Littlefield, Adams & Company: 1969

*The New Age of Banking* by George Sterne, Profit Ideas: 1981

*Polk's World Bank Directory,* R. L. Polk and Company (semiannual directory listing banks by city, state, and foreign country)

*Your Career in Banking,* American Bankers Association: 1980

**PERIODICALS**

*ABA Banking Journal* (monthly), 345 Hudson Street, New York, NY 10014

*American Banker* (daily), One State Street Plaza, New York, NY 10004

*The Banker's Magazine* (bimonthly), Warren, Gorham, and Lamont, Inc., 210 South Street, Boston, MA 02111

*Bank News* (monthly), 912 Baltimore Avenue, Kansas City, MO 64105

## Professional Associations

American Bankers Association
1120 Connecticut Avenue, N.W.
Washington, DC 20036

Consumer Bankers Association
1725 K Street, N.W.
Washington, DC 20006

National Association of Bank Women
111 East Wacker Drive
Chicago, IL 60601

United States League of Savings Associations
111 East Wacker Drive
Chicago, IL 60601

# INTERVIEWS

**Louise D'Imperio, Age 22**
**Operations Analyst**
**Chase Manhattan Bank, New York, NY**

My association with Chase began while I was a student at Villano-
va University. During summer breaks, I was a member of the
apprenticeship management training program, which places
undergraduates in operations. The program provides quality relief
for full-time employees who take vacations.

I worked in the interbank compensation department, which is
responsible for the settlement of funds transfer errors. I worked in
the staff support section, which supports the production line. I
began by doing simple clerical functions, but later became involved in numbers crunching for production tracking reports. In
my final summer, I was an inquiry clerk. My responsibility was to
take customer and other bank questions over the phone and via
telex and inform the individual of the outcome of the compensation
case or reconcile any errors made in settling the case.

In that department I started from the ground up. After three
summers, I really knew how a case was initiated and processed,
and I had a knowledge of the problems that can arise. But after I

graduated in May 1983 I wanted a job outside of bank operations. I have a B.S. in business administration with a concentration in marketing. I wanted a marketing-oriented job and I wanted to be involved in product positioning.

Because I had contacts at Chase, I was able to bypass the normal channels that graduates go through. I looked outside of banking, and mailed résumés to various departments at Chase. Among others, I got a response from Chase international operations and systems.

I chose the position in international operations and systems because I felt that a job in office automation would open up an interesting career path. I knew very little about the field of office automation, but was very interested in it. I work in a division that is concerned with office automation in the international section—more specifically, smaller Chase branches abroad. I'm involved in the marketing and support function of the division, which markets office automation products internally. We want to increase the productivity of individual branches, and we want to increase the use of our products. Our work involves training, consultation, and the development of customized software.

The brunt of my work is project-oriented. Right now I'm working on a project that examines what office automation may do for one of Chase's small subsidiaries. I also edit an office automation newsletter, which takes up about 40 percent of my time, and have written documentation for some of the software developed by our group.

I knew nothing about office automation when I started this job; I actually thought that it involved only word processing. Office automation goes way beyond word processing to include a variety of technologies. My background in operations was not a requirement for this job, but it has made it easier to view the workings of the bank. It also showed me how much I still have to learn about banking. I enjoy my job and I like being involved with technologies that have a definite impact on productivity.

**Jayne Geisler, Age 32**
**Vice President, Market and Financial Planning**
**Chemical Bank, New York, NY**

After receiving a B.A. degree in mathematics and French in 1973 from the State University College of New York at Potsdam, I entered the M.S. teaching program at Boston College, which combined coursework with a part-time teaching position in high school mathematics. Finding teaching unchallenging and realizing my abilities would be better utilized in the business environment, I entered banking, an industry where I felt I could capitalize on my quantitative background

I joined Chemical Bank in 1974 as a financial analyst in the finance, then control, division. My responsiblities included cost accounting and financial management reporting for the consumer banking and upstate regions of the metropolitan (New York) division. Specifically this consisted of preparing, analyzing, and monitoring the financial performance of these business segments against budget and prior years, plus the development of unit and product costs of various banking services. The work was entirely hands-on, with no formal training program, and provided me with a broad understanding of the mechanics of the banking industry.

In 1977 I transferred to the controller's area of the metropolitan division where my duties expanded to include perormance reporting and analysis for the commercial as well as consumer lending areas of the division, acting as a liaison with these areas, plus coordinating their annual budgets. In addition, I was charged with designing and implementing a management information system for evaluating the financial performance of these business segments against budget.

Since 1975 I had been working toward my M.B.A. in finance at night from New York University. Coming from a nonbusiness educational background, I felt that it was apparent that an M.B.A. was necessary to enhance my professional development and my future career goals. It provided me with an understanding of the interrelationships among the key business ingredients—finance, economics, marketing, management, and accounting—which I thought necessary to be more effective in my job. As a result, I am of the opinion that an M.B.A. is an excellent degree for enhancing one's background, especially for those with a liberal arts education. However, I strongly believe that business school is more meaningful and relevant to those who have had prior work experience, as there exists a context in which to augment the course of study.

Upon completion of my M.B.A. in February 1979 I entered the bank's commercial credit training program in order to be a part of the bank's basic business—lending—and to round out my banking experience. I was assigned to the district specializing in the garment/textile/entertainment industries. Handling a portfolio of small business and middle market customers was a challenge. I analyzed and determined credit needs, structured deals, and provided cash management servicing.

Late in 1980 I was asked to join the division's strategic planning unit, which was then undergoing expansion. After a little more than a year as deputy department head, I was promoted to director of the unit, which is my current position. Planning has become increasingly important due to the deregulation of the banking industry. "What do we do now? Where do we want to be in five years? What new products/services should we offer?" These are just some of the challenges facing us as we anticipate the changes in banking law and the movements of our competition. In view of this changing environment created by deregulation, I began working toward a law degree to further supplement my background and experience.

Banking is experiencing tremendous growth and change—it's a whole new ballgame—evolving into a fully integrated financial services industry. The competition not only includes banking institutions, but has expanded to comprise brokerage and investment houses, retailers, high-tech companies, conglomerates, and so forth. As a result, those individuals seeking to enter the industry will need to be sales-oriented and well-rounded in financial services. Banking, finance, and credit will provide the basis, but securities, insurance, and other financial services will play key parts in the banking financial supermarket.

---

# BROADCASTING

Ever since radio station KDKA started sending its programs to the general public in 1920 from a rooftop in Pittsburgh, broadcasting has become—and remains—the quickest and most widespread medium of mass communications. The country's 9000 radio stations and nearly 800 commercial television broadcast stations, plus public radio and television and cable TV, need a steady supply of employees willing to work long and hard, whether on the air, behind a desk, or out selling time in the business community. In both branches of the broadcast media, if you're not cut out for long hours, intense pressure, and teamwork, don't apply. A willingness to relocate, particularly in the early stages of your career, is another important consideration.

Most radio stations choose a particular segment of the population as their target audience and tailor all their programming to that group: news/talk; MOR (middle of the road, a mixture of news, talk, and music); religious; special music such as rock, country, jazz, or classical. It is estimated that 10 to 15 percent of radio stations are now completely automated, playing reels of tape-recorded music hour after hour—but they still require news-casts that are locally developed.

For political science or history majors, the most relevant area in commercial broadcasting is the news; but challenging opportuni-ties can also be found in programming-production.

In the television industry, the networks, who were first on the scene, remain the giants of the industry, along with their local affiliates. Their job opportunities are the most coveted in the business. Independent stations rely primarily on old movies and syndicated reruns, but they still need talented news people. Public Broadcasting Service (PBS) stations have become an increasingly attractive career option for job-hunters because of the growing amount of station-generated programming, much of which gets national exposure through the PBS system.

In the last five years, as more and more homes were wired for cable television, opportunities have opened up for both ex-perienced and inexperienced news reporters and anchors and pro-duction and programming staffers.

Graduates entering the broadcast field may have majored in any number of subjects. If your primary interest is news, a journalism degree is advisable, but a good political science or history back-ground and an understanding of the political, social, and economic underpinnings of the news can be impressive. For most other jobs, employers want people who have demonstrated their interest in the medium through internships or summer jobs, or by independently developing, directing, or producing radio shows or video seg-ments. Good reporting, writing, and editing skills and the ability to meet tight deadlines are essential.

## Job Outlook

*Job Openings Will Grow:*   As fast as average in radio; faster than average in TV.

*Competition For Jobs:*   Keen

*New Job Opportunities:*   In radio, the Federal Communications Commission (FCC) has recently dropped a variety of programming regulations to give stations much freer rein. An expected relaxing of other standards could mean the rise of as many as 1400 new FM stations in the next several years, and still more jobs will be created if the plan to expand the top end of the AM dial is put into effect.

In the meantime, look for new job opportunities at syndicated radio services, which provide and distribute a wide array of recorded materials and whose number keeps growing. The latest among these are the specialized networks, such as Hispanic News Service, headquartered in Washington, DC, and National Black Network, headquartered in New York, NY.

Low power television was recently approved by the FCC. These new stations will broadcast in a very limited geographic area and will be accessible to community and minority groups. They should be an excellent source of valuable entry-level experience, because their small staffs will allow individual members to try their hand at a variety of station functions.

## Geographic Job Index

The corporate offices of both radio and TV networks are in New York, NY, and Los Angeles, CA. New York is the home of the news bureaus and most daytime soap operas, whereas the majority of network entertainment programming originates on the West Coast. Important network television desks also operate in Chicago, IL, and Washington, DC. However, most job openings exist outside these centers, in local broadcasting.

### Who the Employers Are

MAJOR TELEVISION NETWORKS (ABC, CBS, NBC) employ thousands in their corporate offices, but job opportunities there are extremely limited for recent grads. An entry-level job at a network often requires the applicant to have professional experience or an advanced degree in business or law. Other jobs for recent graduates are usually secretarial or of the go-fer variety. Advancement is possible but difficult.

COMMERCIAL TELEVISION STATIONS operate across the country; there are approximately 780 such stations. The networks each have about 200 affiliates; some are directly owned by the parent network; others operate independently. In either case, each affiliate has its own hiring policies and procedures, as do the country's 180 independent stations.

NATIONAL RADIO NETWORKS (ABC, CBS, NBC) provide programming for their affiliate stations and, along with the other major networks—the Mutual Broadcasting System, AP Radio Network, UPI Audio, and RKO Radio Network—provide extensive coverage of national and international events and a variety of features to member stations.

STATE OR REGIONAL RADIO NETWORKS are associations of broadcast stations within a state or region that supply news of that area to member stations. These networks are the Florida News Network, Texas State Network, Oklahoma News Network, and the Arkansas, Georgia, Louisiana, Mississippi, and Missouri Networks.

The goal of many graduates is to land a job in one of the approximately 50 major television markets, which serve at least 500,000 viewing households, or the 25 largest U.S. cities that have a population of at least 1,300,000 and make up the major radio markets. Major market stations attract top-level, experienced people; competition for the relatively few entry-level jobs is intense.

MEDIUM AND SMALL MARKET RADIO STATIONS are located throughout the country. Cities with populations of between 500,000 and 1,000,000 are considered medium markets. Small market radio stations are found in communities of under 50,000, and nearly 40 percent of all radio stations in the United States fall into this latter category.

INDEPENDENT RADIO SYNDICATORS produce and distribute programming. Most of this production is music, but news, sports, and other features are also packaged. These services provide job opportunities primarily for graduates interested in programming and production.

PUBLIC TELEVISION STATIONS, numbering 300, make up the PBS system. They deliver educational, information, and artistic programming and operate in 49 states (all but Montana) and four U.S. territories, making PBS the world's most extensive television system. Each station does its own hiring, and staff size depends on the amount of production done at the station. However, very few public stations have the personnel or resources required for extensive production, so most PBS programming originates from the following five stations: WGBH (Boston, MA), WNET (New York, NY), WETA (Washington, DC), KCET (Los Angeles, CA), and WTTW (Chicago, IL). PBS headquarters in Washington, DC, is a small operation and employs primarily administrative staff. The radio counterpart of PBS is National Public Radio, with more than 180 stations across the United States. Here, too, hiring is done by individual stations, and programming is generated to the extent that station resources will allow. Other programming—such as NPR's "Morning Edition" and "All Things Considered"— comes from their Washington, DC, headquarters.

*Major Employers*

The eight largest U.S. television broadcast markets, those with more than 1,500,000 viewing households, are listed here in order of size. Each of these cities also has a number of independent stations in addition to the network affiliates and PBS stations listed below.

   1. NEW YORK, NY
   AFFILIATE: WABC (ABC), WCBS (CBS), WNBC
      (NBC)
   PBS: WNET

   2. LOS ANGELES, CA
   AFFILIATE: KABC (ABC), KNBC (NBC), KNXT
      (CBS)
   PBS: KCET, KLCS

3. CHICAGO, IL
AFFILIATE: WBBM (CBS), WLS (ABC), WMAQ
    (NBC)
PBS: WTTW

4. PHILADELPHIA, PA
AFFILIATE: KYW (NBC), WCAU (CBS), WPVI (ABC)
PBS: WHYY

5. SAN FRANCISCO, CA
AFFILIATE: KGO (ABC), KPIX (CBS), KRON (NBC)
PBS: KQED

6. BOSTON, MA
AFFILIATE: WBZ (NBC), WCBV (ABC), WNEV
    (CBS)
PBS: WGBH

7. DETROIT, MI
AFFILIATE: WDIV (NBC), WJBK (CBS), WXYZ
    (ABC)
PBS: WKAR, WTVS

8. WASHINGTON, DC
AFFILIATE: WDVM (CBS), WJLA (ABC), WRC
    (NBC)
PBS: WETA


The following cities are the top 25 radio markets, which each have at least 1,300,000 listeners.

1. New York, NY
2. Los Angeles, CA
3. Chicago, IL
4. San Francisco, CA
5. Philadelphia, PA

6. Detroit, MI
7. Boston, MA
8. Houston, TX
9. Washington, DC
10. Dallas-Fort Worth, TX
11. Miami-Fort Lauderdale-Hollywood, FL
12. Naussau-Suffolk, Long Island, NY
13. St. Louis, MO
14. Pittsburgh, PA
15. Baltimore, MD
16. Seattle-Everett-Tacoma, WA
17. Minneapolis-St. Paul, MN
18. Atlanta, GA
19. Anaheim-Santa Ana-Garden Grove, CA
20. San Diego, CA
21. Cleveland, OH
22. Tampa-St. Petersburg, FL
23. Denver-Boulder, CO
24. Phoenix, AZ
25. Milwaukee-Racine, WI

## How to Break into the Field

Knowing someone who can hire you or tell you about openings and recommend you is your best bet, but prior experience is the key. Investigate internship opportunities at a local station, or volunteer to work during summers and weekends. (Public television and radio stations are often the most receptive to volunteer help.) And get involved with your campus radio or TV station. Your best chance for a first job is at a small station. Send a carefully thought-out and well-written letter to the general manager of the station you've chosen and request an interview. Follow up with a phone call.

The once-rapid growth in programming services for the cable television industry slowed somewhat in 1983. Some services proved to be unprofitable and have folded or merged with more successful ones. Job openings, where they do occur, are often taken by experienced professionals. If you are willing to work part-time or as a free-lancer instead of waiting for a staff opening, you may stand a chance of finding a job in this area.

Most large radio stations hold newswriting examinations, which applicants have likened to taking the bar exam. The writer is given two hours to go over 12 hours' worth of wire copy and create a five-minute radio newscast from it. Such an exam should not be undertaken until you have a considerable amount of experience under your belt.

If you're female, or a member of a minority group, you can get help in finding positions in commercial broadcasting by writing to:

NAB Employment Clearinghouse
1771 N Street, N.W.
Washington, DC 20036

If you'd like to work in public radio, the National Association of Educational Broadcasters operates PACT (People and Careers in Telecommunications), a free, nationwide employment service. Write to:

National Association of Educational Broadcasters PACT
1346 Connecticut Avenue, N.W.
Washington, DC 20036

Competition for on-air jobs in both radio and television is intense. Hopefuls must have not only good reporting skills, but a clear speaking voice, an attractive appearance (for television), and an appealing presence as well. Starting in a small market is a must. Advancement comes by moving to larger and larger markets, and only the very best make it to the network level.

Much more plentiful are behind-the-scenes reporting jobs: writing and editing copy, preparing background research, and keeping and updating files on developing stories. These jobs can be just as exciting and demanding as those of reporters and anchors and provide better stepping-stones to management positions.

# NEWS

By far the best opportunities for political science or history majors in broadcasting exist in radio and television news departments. The news department is often the largest at a station, but job opportunities are often awarded first to those with a journalism background. However, here your background may give you a competitive edge.

Radio news departments receive national and international news over a teletype machine from the news services: Associated Press (AP) and United Press International (UPI). Less frequently the news is sent as an audio feed by broadcast lines to local stations.

For local stories, the stations fend for themselves. Armed with a tape recorder and microphone, their reporters go wherever the action is. As a reporter, you'll interview people at the scene, take notes, and tape-record interviews and meetings before writing a story summarizing the event and editing the tape for appropriate quotes to thread into your story. You'll write, edit, and deliver the story back at the station if there's still time before the next newscast; otherwise you'll write the story on the spot and dictate it over the phone into a machine at the station.

Most radio stations broadcast the news at least once every hour. Although news jobs are extremely difficult to get, the total number of these jobs has increased because of the growing number of stations broadcasting all news 24 hours a day.

## Qualifications

*Personal:*   Natural curiosity. A capacity for hard work and long hours. Ability to handle pressure and deadlines. For on-air work, good diction. A voice and delivery that convey warmth and authority.

*Professional:*   Television: Reporting and writing skills. Typing required; knowledge of video display terminals (VDTs) helpful, as these are becoming more common in TV newsrooms. Ability to work accurately with speed, usually under pressure of a deadline.

**RADIO:**    Ability to write for the ear. Sound news judgment. Good reporting, editing, and rewriting skills. Ability to edit tape.

## Career Paths

**TELEVISION:**    (These apply primarily to off-camera personnel.)

| LEVEL | JOB TITLE | EXPERIENCE NEEDED |
|---|---|---|
| Entry | Desk assistant | College degree |
| 2 | Newswriter | 1-2 years |
| 3 | Assistant news producer | 6-8 years |
| 4 | News producer | 10-12 years |

**RADIO**

| LEVEL | JOB TITLE | EXPERIENCE NEEDED |
|---|---|---|
| Entry | Desk assistant, network radio<br>Reporter, small network | College degree |
| 2 | Reporter, medium market | 2 years |
| 3 | Reporter, major market<br>News director, small market | 5 years |
| 4 | News director, major market<br>Reporter, network | 10+ years |

## Job Responsibilities

## Entry Level

THE BASICS: Clerical duties. Maintaining news service machines. Collecting and distributing audio feeds to news editors and writers. Helping prepare sports scores and weather round-ups. Checking facts. General messenger duties for the news department.

MORE CHALLENGING DUTIES: Television: Writing or rewriting copy. Simple editing of copy to conform to time limitations. Reviewing film clips. Radio: Interviewing sources. Putting together an early morning newscast by clearing the news wire machines of copy that has "moved" during the night and pulling stories for use on the upcoming newscasts, listening to audio feeds, phoning police and hospitals for overnight news and updates, then writing and editing the newscast from the material gathered.

## Moving Up

As an assistant, you learn the daily routine of the newsroom, the style of its scripted copy, and the discipline to write under deadline. Once you reach the level of newswriter, you write the actual copy and you may edit other writers' stories. In radio, your next job will no doubt be reporting.

Several years of writing or reporting experience may lead to the position of assistant news producer in television, which combines organizational and managerial skills with critical judgment. In radio, a promotion possibility is becoming a news director, if you've proved yourself to be an ace reporter and, in addition, have managerial know-how. At most radio stations, the news director determines the overall news policy of the station, supervises the news personnel, and previews the newscasts to ensure that they're a satisfying blend of local, national, and international concerns. The news director also may serve as a reporter and newscaster.

In television, the assistant news producer, in cooperation with the news producer, oversees the daily routine, assigns stories, and decides which stories get precedence. These senior people also have the last word in the selection of accompanying film.

# PROGRAMMING-PRODUCTION

Because the networks are responsible for the majority of daytime and evening programming, their program staffs number in the hundreds. Major programming areas beyond the news and documentary departments—sports, morning talk shows, soap operas, children's programs, and prime-time shows—have individual staffs. The television network programming and production staffs conceive, plan, and create most shows except for prime-time shows and made-for-TV movies, which they commission or purchase from independent production houses. In radio, all on-air material except for news is selected, prepared, or purchased by the programming department. Independent and network-affiliate TV stations still do a sizable amount of programming themselves, and this is where many job openings can be found. In radio, FCC regulations oblige the station to provide public service programming, and this may well be a place where your background is particularly apt. In addition, the surging popularity of talk shows has increased the number of people needed to plan and produce that type of programming. In fact, a growing number of major AM stations have become all-talk, and most stations do at least some talk show programming that is often aired early on Sunday mornings or late on Sunday evenings. Hosting a show, lining up guests, and developing a formula for talk programming is often the job of the director of public affairs. Although you may be given one of these responsibilities at a small station on your first job, you'll have to become more seasoned in programming before going on to a similar position at a medium or major market station.

Production staffers may develop program ideas, prepare scripts, work with free-lance writers and on-air talent, and edit the show after taping. In radio, if you're a talented behind-the-scenes programming person, you could be hired as an associate producer, helping the producer to conceive, develop, and produce a show; conducting interviews; writing scripts; and editing tapes. If you demonstrate taste and can forecast trends, you'll be ready to move up to producer, a position in which you'll choose the people to be interviewed, handle all the business arrangements, supervise production personnel, and act as overall manager of the program. Success in any of these areas may land you a job as program director, responsible for coordinating and presenting the complete daily programming schedule.

The television production assistant is, in many ways, an apprentice. Opportunities for advancement depend on the size of the station and the complexity of its operations. As assistant producer, you might work on a specific regular program or on various specials. You typically then become a producer, working in ever larger markets on more involved programming. Or you might move on to an administrative position, such as production director or program director.

## ADDITIONAL INFORMATION

### Salaries

Network people make the highest salaries. At both independent and network-affiliated stations, the larger the market, the higher the pay. Those who work in public television or radio make less than their counterparts at commercial stations. The following figures, compiled by the National Association of Broadcasters in a 1983 survey, represent the average salary nationwide.

**RADIO**

| | |
|---|---|
| News editor | $15,250 |
| News reporter | $15,294 |
| News announcer | $15,320 |
| News director | $19,385 |

**TELEVISION**

| | |
|---|---|
| News reporter | $20,497 |
| News producer | $37,558 |
| News anchor | $42,348 |

## Working Conditions

*Hours:*   Radio: Many radio stations operate 24 hours a day, seven days a week, so in news expect to work long hours. As a neophyte, you'll often be assigned the worst shifts (midnight to 8 A.M.; 4:30 A.M. to noon), and to weekend and holiday assignments. Be prepared for overtime. Television: News must be reported up until the end of the 11 P.M. newscast seven days a week, and into the early hours on the networks' late-night programs.

*Environment:*   In general, the atmosphere is noisy, cluttered, and hectic, with ringing phones and loud talk. Office privacy is a luxury reserved for senior staff members. Because reporters are under continuous deadline pressure, it's a high-tension, fast-moving atmosphere.

*Workstyle:*   As a reporter, you're on your feet and out of the office much of the day, tracking down stories. The rest of the time you're in the newsroom editing and rewriting stories that come in over the wires.

*Travel:*   Only network-level reporters do a significant amount of out-of-town travel, and they are usually based in major cities or even abroad.

## Extracurricular Activities/Work Experience

Campus newspaper, publications, radio or television
station—reporting and writing, production,
announcing

Volunteer—local public radio or television station

Sports events—announcing

Drama club—directing, acting, technical crew

Debate club—participant

## Internships

The International Radio and Television Society's internship program is open only to junior and senior communications majors. Investigate summer and part-time opportunities by contacting local radio and television stations and cable systems. Although some stations pay interns, most take them only as volunteers.

## Recommended Reading

**BOOKS**

*Anchorwoman* by Jessica Savitch, Berkeley Publishing: 1983

*Before the Colors Faded* by Harry Reasoner, Quill Publications: 1983

*Broadcasting Yearbook* published by Broadcasting Publications, Inc. (lists names and addresses of radio stations, national and regional networks, and major program producers)

*Good Evening Everybody* by Lowell Thomas, Avon Books: 1977

*Larry King* by Larry King and Emily Yoffe, Simon & Schuster: 1982

*The Making of a Woman Reporter: This Is Judy Woodruff at the White House* by Judy Woodruff and Kathy Maxa, Addison-Wesley Publishing Company: 1982

*Not So Wild a Dream* by Eric Severeid, Atheneum Publishers: 1978

*On the Radio: With Harden and Weaver* by Frank Harden, et al., William Morrow and Company: 1983

*Over the Wire and on TV: CBS and UPI in Campaign '80* by Michael J. Robinson, Russel Sage Foundation: 1983

*Radio in the Television Age* by Peter Fornatale and Joshua Mills, Overlook Press: 1983

*Television Digest's Cable and Station Coverage Atlas,* Revised, TV and Cable Factbook: 1982

**PERIODICALS**
*Billboard* (weekly), Billboard Publications, 1 Astor Plaza, 1515 Broadway, New York, NY 10036

*Broadcasting* (weekly), Broadcasting Publications, Inc., 1735 DeSales Street, N.W., Washington, DC 20036
*Cable Age* (biweekly), Television Editorial Corporation, 1270 Avenue of the Americas, New York, NY 10020

*Cable Television Business* (weekly), Cardiff Publishing Company, 6430 Yosemite Street, Englewood, CO 80111

*Inside TV* (monthly), McFadden-Bartell Corporation, 215 Lexington Avenue, New York, NY 10016

*Radio & Records* (weekly), 1930 Century Park West, Los Angeles, CA 90067

*Television Radio Age* (biweekly), 1270 Avenue of the Americas, New York, NY 10020

*Variety* (weekly), Variety, Inc., 154 West 46th Street, New York, NY 10036

## Professional Associations

American Women in Radio and Television
1321 Connecticut Avenue, N.W.
Washington, DC 20036

International Radio and Television Society
420 Lexington Avenue
New York, NY 10170

The National Association of Broadcasters
1771 N Street, N.W.
Washington, DC 20036

The National Radio Broadcasters Association
1705 DeSales Street, N.W.
Washington, DC 20036

# INTERVIEWS

**Mark Scheerer, Age 34**
**Roving Correspondent**
**ABC Radio News, New York, NY**

Although I majored in journalism in college, I never took a broadcasting course. I didn't even work at the campus radio station. I was too shy to speak in front of a microphone—or so I thought until I got my first job at a small FM station in Sylvania, Ohio. I worked as a disc jockey and a news broadcaster there before I was named news director for a larger station, WIOT, in Ohio.

As news director at major stations in Cincinnati, Philadelphia, and Chicago, I've covered five national political conventions, White House news conferences, the emergency at Three Mile Island, the visits of the Pope, the Winter Olympics, the World Series, and the Super Bowl.

For several years, I worked the morning drive shift (6 to 10 A.M.). It's difficult to be creative, funny, and compelling on the air at an early hour. But that's the time when most people want their daily dose of news. When you have to get up at four o'clock in the morning, your social life is terrible.

It took me 11 years to land the radio job of my dreams—working as a roving correspondent for ABC News—but it was worth it. Had I been tied down with a relationship or marriage, I might not have been able to relocate as often as I did, which is what most people in my business do in order to move up to bigger and better markets.

I think I have the greatest job in radio news—I go wherever a big story or event is happening, and I get to tell it to hundreds of thousands of young Americans. While most of the stories I work on are exciting, I'm also required to be on the scene whenever necessary, which may mean showing up at 8 A.M. to cover a story on dioxin contamination in Hoboken, New Jersey.

If you want to work in radio, get as much firsthand experience as you can while you're still in school—at the campus station or a local one. Take a wide variety of courses so you're knowledgeable about many subjects. And be persistent in your search to get into a radio news slot. It's competitive, but if you're willing to start out at a small station and build on your experience, you're bound to go places.

**John Carver, Age 41**
**Director of Grant Support**
**WGBH Public Television, Boston, MA**

The highlights of my job are selling a quality product and working with people who really enjoy their work. I'm surrounded by very bright people who want to be here. There's a team spirit at WGBH that I have never known on other jobs.

I'm responsible for finding corporate sponsors or underwriters for programs my station produces for national delivery through PBS. My clients are high-level corporate people, usually close to senior vice presidential level. To them, I'm not so much a salesman as I am a broker, bringing two interested parties together. My job is to travel to cities where corporate headquarters are located to see if I can interest them in associating their names with a production. Usually, their company has expressed interest in public television, and my job is to find the right product for them. I talk frequently with our programming department to try to match up something that's in the works with a particular company's needs.

I like to define our product as the Rolls-Royce of TV programming. Those of us in public television see ourselves as part of a widely accepted alternative to standard and predictable commercial fare. We make less money than our counterparts in network or local TV. But in my department, there's more opportunity than in others to earn a good living because we're paid on a salary plus commission basis.

# DEPARTMENT STORE RETAILING

ONSUMERS generally take for granted that they will always find their favorite department stores brimming with merchandise. Unnoticed by most customers, a large, talented staff works long, hard hours to keep the shelves filled, the selection varied, the stores beautiful, and the business of retailing running smoothly. Retailing is an industry in which brains and diligence can take you to high levels of decision-making years before your contemporaries in other fields have reached similar positions of responsibility.

Graduates of virtually any discipline may enter department store retailing. Prospective employers are looking for demonstrated capacity to learn and make quick, sound judgments and are less interested in academic backgrounds. You must be flexible, comfortable with people, self-disciplined, and highly motivated—and a sense of humor certainly does not hurt. Retailing is a high-pressure profession where no slow seasons exist—only busy and busier, with the November-December pre-Christmas rush being the most hectic time of all. Prior retail experience, even a summer spent behind a cash register, is a plus; some retailers won't consider candidates without it.

Most entry-level jobs are in merchandising, an area further divided into:

- **Store Management**
- **Buying**

Your job in merchandising begins with a training period of six months to a year. Some trainees divide their time between classroom learning and work experience, others train entirely on the job. Generally, the larger the retailer, the more formalized the training. Whether you enter the field via store management or buying depends primarily on the employer. Many stores separate these functions beginning at the entry level; you must choose which path you prefer. Other stores will introduce all new merchandising personnel to buying and later allow those interested in and qualified for management to move up. The opposite arrangement, moving into buying at some later stage, also occurs, although infrequently.

The modern store is reaping the benefits of the technological revolution. Point-of-sale computer terminals are replacing mechanical cash registers; these automatically compute sales, taxes, and discounts and simplify inventory control by keeping sales records. Computers are also used for credit records and tracking sales forecasts.

Retailing is vulnerable to downturns in the economy, but it's one of the first industries to bounce back after a recession. As a highly profit-oriented business, it's hectic and competitive. The customer's satisfaction and loyalty to the store are very important, which means that you must tolerate and even pamper people whom you may not like. In retailing, the unexpected is the order of the day; you can expect to feel pressured, but seldom unchallenged.

## Job Outlook

*Job Openings Will Grow:*   As fast as average

*Competition for Jobs:*  Keen

In merchandising, the most competition exists in buying; this area has fewer openings, tends to pay a bit better, and has an aura of glamour about it.

*New Job Opportunities:*  An exciting new technological development, still in experimental form, that may change retailing in the next decade is video retailing. A select number of communities now have a two-way cable television system through which viewers may receive and send information to a broadcasting center. Viewers can order goods seen on the screen by typing their selections on a keyboard. Video retailing is still in developmental form, but those entering retailing should be aware of its potential as a new job area.

## Geographic Job Index

The location of retail jobs parallels the distribution of the general population; stores operate where customers live. As an up-and-coming executive in a retail chain, expect to work in a city or suburban area. Most new store construction in the coming years is expected to take place in revitalizing city cores. Department stores are found across the country, with the highest concentration of jobs in the Northeast, Midwest and West Coast.

If your interest is buying, your geographic options are more limited. For many department store chains, most or all buying takes place in a few key markets, notably New York, NY.

## Who the Employers Are

A retailer is, in its simplest definition, a third party who sells a producer's goods to a consumer for a profit. The retailing industry as a whole comprises a wide variety of stores of different sizes with different personnel needs. Management personnel are sought by all major retail firms, including grocery, drug, specialty, and variety store chains, but because the most varied opportunities are found in department stores, this chapter focuses on this sector of retailing.

*Major Employers*

Allied Stores Corporation, New York, NY
  Bonwit Teller
  Field's
  Jordan Marsh
  Stern's

Carter Hawley Hale Stores, Los Angeles, CA
  Bergdorf Goodman
  The Broadway
  John Wanamaker
  Neiman-Marcus

Dayton Hudson Corporation, Minneapolis, MN
  Dayton's
  Diamond's

Federated Department Stores, New York, NY
  Abraham & Straus
  Bullock's
  Filene's
  Foley's
  I. Magnin
  Rich's

R.H. Macy & Company, New York, NY

Montgomery Ward & Company, Chicago, IL

J. C. Penney Company, New York, NY

Sears, Roebuck & Company, Chicago, IL

### How to Break into the Field

Your best bet is on-campus interviews. Major retailers actively recruit on college campuses. This is the most accessible way to most potential employers. Don't hesitate, however, to contact employers directly, especially if you want to work for a smaller operation. Read the business section of your newspaper regularly to find out about store expansions, the addition of new stores or locations, and other developments in retailing that can provide important clues to new job openings. Keep in mind that retail or selling experience of any kind will increase your chances of getting hired.

### International Job Opportunities

Extremely limited. Opportunities to live abroad exist at the corporate level of a few international chains.

# STORE MANAGEMENT

If you're a "people person," consider the store management side of merchandising. You'll be responsible for handling the needs of staff and customers.

The job of store management personnel, even at entry level, entails making decisions on your own. But since decisions often have to be made on the spot and involve balancing the interests of both customers and the store, your mistakes are likely to be highly visible. Whether you manage the smallest department or a very large store, you must always keep the bottom line—making a profit—in mind when making decisions.

During training, you will work with experienced managers and will be moved throughout the store to observe all aspects of merchandising. If you're quick to learn and demonstrate management potential, you'll soon be made manager of a small department or assistant manager of a large one. You will have a fair amount of autonomy, but you must stick to store standards and implement policies determined by higher level management.

## Qualifications

*Personal:*   Ability to learn quickly. Enormous enthusiasm. The flexibility to handle a constantly changing schedule. Willingness to work weekends, holidays, and nights.

*Professional:*   Demonstrated leadership ability. Ability to work with figures, finances, inventories, and quotas. A sense of diplomacy.

## Career Paths

| LEVEL | JOB TITLE | EXPERIENCE NEEDED |
|---|---|---|
| Entry | Department manager trainee | College degree |
| 2 | Group department manager | 2-3 years |
| 3 | Assistant store manager | 5-10 years |
| 4 | Store manager | 8-12 years |

## Job Responsibilities

## Entry Level

THE BASICS:   Handling staff scheduling. Dealing with customer complaints. Doing plenty of paperwork.

MORE CHALLENGING DUTIES:   Monitoring and motivating your sales staff. Assisting in the selection of merchandise for your department. Making decisions and solving problems.

## Moving Up

Advancement in store management depends on how well you shoulder responsibility and take advantage of opportunities to learn. Effectively leading your staff, moving merchandise, and, above all, turning a profit will secure your promotion into higher levels.

Your first management position will be overseeing a small department, handling greater volumes of money and merchandise. The group department manager directs several department managers, coordinating store operations on a larger scale. From here you might progress to assistant store manager and store manager; this last position is, in many respects, similar to running a private business. The best may then go on to the corporate level.

Relocation is often necessary in order to win promotions. Switching store locations every three years or so is not uncommon. However, depending on the chain, a change of workplace need not require a change of address; often stores are within easy driving distance of each other. But the larger the chain, the greater the possibility that you'll have to move to a different city to further your career.

# BUYING

Do you fantasize about a shopping spree in the world's fashion capitals? A few lucky buyers, after years of work and experience, are paid to do just that when they're sent to Hong Kong, Paris, or Milan to select new lines of merchandise. Most do not make it to such heights, but on a smaller scale, this is the business of buying.

A buyer decides which goods will be available in a store. Buyers authorize merchandise purchases from wholesalers and set the retail prices. A sensitivity to changing trends, tastes, and styles and an ability to understand and forecast the preference of your own store's customers is crucial. Buyers must also maintain standards of quality while keeping within certain ranges of affordability.

The buyer who works for a discount department store faces a particularly tough job. Obtaining lower-than-average prices for quality merchandise is a real challenge and requires an unerring eye and an ability to negotiate with sellers.

Astute buying translates into profits for the store and advancement for your career. Learning how to spend large sums of money wisely takes practice. Fortunately, as a new buyer you can afford to make a few mistakes, even an occasional expensive one, without jeopardizing your career. A good buyer takes calculated risks, and as you gain experience more of your choices will succeed.

During training, you'll work immediately as an assistant to an experienced buyer. The trainee progresses by observing, asking questions, and offering to take on appropriate responsibilities.

## Qualifications

*Personal:*   An interest in changing trends and fashions. An ability to work with a wide variety of personalities. A willingness to channel creativity into a commercial enterprise.

*Professional:*   Financial and negotiating know-how. Organizational skills. Good judgment in spotting trends and evaluating products.

### Career Paths

| LEVEL | JOB TITLE | EXPERIENCE NEEDED |
|---|---|---|
| Entry | Assistant or junior buyer | College degree and store training |
| 2 | Buyer (small lines) | 2-5 years |
| 3 | Buyer (large lines) | 4-10 years |
| 4 | Corporate merchandise manager | 15+ years |

## Job Responsibilities

### Entry Level

**THE BASICS:** Assisting your supervising buyer. Placing orders and speaking with manufacturers by phone. Supervising the inspection and unpacking of new merchandise and overseeing its distribution.

**MORE CHALLENGING DUTIES:** Becoming acquainted with various manufacturers' lines. Considering products for purchase. Evaluating your store's needs. Keeping an eye on the competition.

### Moving Up

Advancement depends on proof of your ability to judge customer needs and to choose saleable goods. The only purchases closely scrutinized by higher authorities are those inconsistent with past practices and standards.

After completing your training, you will first buy for a small department, then, as you become seasoned, for larger departments. High-placed buyers make decisions in buying for a key department common to several stores, for an entire state, or possibly for many stores. Your buying plans must always be well coordinated with the needs of store management.

# ADDITIONAL INFORMATION

## Salaries

Entry-level salaries range from $12,000 to $18,000 a year, depending on the employer and the geographic location of the store. Junior buyers tend to be among the best paid entry-level employees.

The following salary ranges show typical annual salaries for experienced retail personnel. In merchandising salaries vary with the size and importance of your department.

| | |
|---|---|
| 2-4 years: | $16,000-24,000 |
| 5-10 years: | $22,000-27,000 |
| 12 years or more: | $25,000 and up |

## Working Conditions

*Hours:*   Most retail personnel work a five-day, 40-hour week, but schedules vary with different positions. In store management, daily shifts are rarely nine to five, because stores are open as many as 12 hours a day, seven days a week. Night, weekend, and holiday duty are unavoidable, especially for newcomers. Operations personnel work similar hours. Buyers have more regular schedules and are rarely asked to work evening and weekend hours.

*Environment:*   In merchandising, your time is divided between the office and the sales floor—more often the latter. Office space at the entry level may or may not be private, depending on the store. Whether you share space or not, expect to be close to the sales floor. Merchandising is no place for those who need absolute privacy and quiet in order to be productive.

*Workstyle:*   In store management, office time is 100 percent work; every valuable moment must be used effectively to keep on top of the paperwork. On the floor you will be busy overseeing the arrangement of merchandise, meeting with your sales staff, and listening to customer complaints. Long hours on your feet will test your patience and endurance, but you can never let the weariness show. In buying, office time is spent with paperwork and calls to manufacturers. You might also review catalog copy and illustrations. On the sales floor, you'll meet with store personnel to see how merchandise is displayed and, most important, to see how the customers are responding. Manufacturers' representatives will visit to show their products, and you might spend some days at manufacturer and wholesaler showrooms. Because these jobs bring you into the public eye, you must be well dressed and meticulously groomed. The generous discounts that employees receive as a fringe benefit help defray the cost of maintaining a wardrobe.

*Travel:* In store management, your responsibility lies with your own department and your own store; travel opportunities are virtually nonexistent, except for some top-level personnel. Buyers, particularly those who live outside major manufacturing centers, may make annual trips to New York, NY, and other key cities. You might also travel to trade shows at which your type of merchandise is displayed.

## Extracurricular Activities/Work Experience

Leadership in campus organizations

Treasurer or financial officer of an organization

Sales position on the yearbook or campus newspaper

Summer or part-time work in any aspect of retailing

## Internships

Arrange internships with individual stores or chains; many are eager to hire interns, preferring students who are in the fall semester of their senior year. Check with your school's placement or internship office or with the store itself in the spring for a fall internship. Summer internships are also available with some stores. Contact the placement office or the personnel departments of individual stores for details.

## Recommended Reading

**BOOKS**

*Buyer's Manual*, National Retail Merchants Association: 1979

*Creative Selling: A Programmed Approach* by R.J. Burley, Addison-Wesley: 1982

*The Retail Revolution: Market Transformation, Investment, and Labor in the Modern Department Store* by Barry Bluestone et al., Auburn House: 1981

*The Woolworths* by James Brough, McGraw-Hill: 1982

**PERIODICALS**

*Advertising Age* (weekly), Crain Communications, 740 North Rush Street, Chicago, IL 60611

*Journal of Retailing* (quarterly), New York University, 202 Tisch Building, New York, NY 10003

*Stores* (monthly), National Retail Merchants Association, 100 West 31st Street, New York, NY 10001

*Women's Wear Daily* (daily), Fairchild Publications, Inc., 7 East 12th Street, New York, NY 10003

## Professional Associations

American Marketing Association
250 South Wacker Drive
Chicago, IL 60606

American Retail Federation
1616 H Street, N.W.
Washington, DC 20006

Association of General Merchandise Chains
1625 I Street, N.W.
Washington, DC 20006

National Retail Merchants Association
100 West 31st Street
New York, NY 10001

# INTERVIEWS

**Carolyn Egan, Age 33**
**Fashion Coordinator**
**Bloomingdale's Department Store, NY**

My first job was far removed from retailing—I taught high school math for a year. But the school environment really didn't excite me and I felt I could get more from a job. I saw an ad for the position of fashion coordinator at a branch of Gimbels' department store. I wasn't planning a career in retailing, but because I kept up with fashion and felt I had a flair for it, I applied. I got the job and enjoyed the work, but that particular branch was not a high-caliber store, and after two years I was ready to move on.

I took a part-time job as an assistant manager at an Ann Taylor store, one of a chain selling women's clothing. At that time I was also going to school to finish an art degree. My job included store management and some limited buying. I wound up managing my own store, but because Ann Taylor has a small management staff, I felt there wasn't enough growth potential. I came to know the man who was doing store design for the chain. He was expanding his operations and needed help, so I went to work with him. I designed store interiors and fixtures, which gave me a whole new perspective on the industry. I have been lucky to see so many sides of retailing, but these job changes also required me to relocate.

When I moved into fashion coordination with Bloomingdale's about seven years ago, I finally found what I had been looking for—a high-powered, high-pressured environment. When I walk into the store each morning I feel that things are moving, happening. That's the fun of retailing.

My responsibility is to work with the buyers, helping them choose the right styles. After you've been in retailing a number of years, you know where fashion has been and you can see where it's going. You decide—really by making educated guesses—what the public will want a year from today. My job includes a lot of travel—usually eight or nine weeks a year. Where there are products abroad, we explore them. That's the only way to keep up with the competition.

In buying we speak of hundreds of dozens, so you must be volume-oriented. You ask, "What does our regular customer want to see?" Then you make a decision that has to be more right than wrong. I work with children's wear, a department that rarely sees radical changes in style. But there are always new trends in color and design, and new products.

One of the toughest parts of my job is training new buyers and helping with their first big buys. They are understandably nervous about spending several hundred thousand dollars. The fashion coordinator is one with buying experience. You offer better advice if you understand the pressure and monetary responsibility of the buyer's job.

Even though I'm in a creative area, business and financial concerns are of the highest importance. You must have a head for business in every retailing job. You want to find beautiful quality products, but if they don't sell, you've failed.

The one drawback to my job is advancement. My talents and experience are best used right where I am now. Unlike the buyers, I really have no place higher to go. But I enjoy my work. I suppose it's like being an artist, and how many artists are really appreciated?

## G. G. Michelson, Age 58
## Senior Vice President for External Affairs
## R. H. Macy & Company, NY

My job is a rather unique one—it had never existed before and was tailored just for me. I represent the company in the community in its relationships with government, and in philanthropy. I was the senior vice president for personnel and labor relations in the New York division before moving into the corporate side about five years ago.

I was given this opportunity because of my long association and familiarity with the company and the business. We have a separate public relations department, and I don't interfere with their plans; rather, I am involved in considerations of corporate policy. For example, I handle difficult shareholder and community questions. We have a substantial philanthropy budget to work with. We want to spend this money creatively, but our charitable actions must be in line with our business decisions. We are primarily concerned with the communities in which our stores are located, because we recognize our obligation to those places in which we make our living.

I was quite young when I graduated from college, so I went on to law school to mature and get that valuable credential—but I never intended to practice law. All along I knew that I wanted to work in labor relations.

I considered manufacturing and some of the heavy industries as potential employers, and I came to realize that retailing as a service industry was far more people-intensive than other businesses. I found that in retailing the personnel function had a great deal more status and received more attention from top management. Looking elsewhere, I noticed that the emphasis was on cost control, not people development.

I went directly into Macy's training program from law school. The training program was and, of course, still is largely devoted to merchandising. I worked in merchandising only for the six months that I trained, but that experience gave me an excellent background for understanding the business and the people in it. In employee relations, I had responsibility for hiring, training, and developing our employees and merchandising talent.

In the past ten years, I have seen a significant change in the kind of graduates entering retailing. We now hire a great many graduates who once would have pursued other careers—graduates certified to teach, for instance—and people with liberal arts backgrounds who once would have gone on to grad school. We have always hired people who have broad educations; we have never been too concerned about a candidate's business background. We develop our talent by training people for top management, so we are looking for the ability to learn and grow. We don't want to have to train a person to think for the first time!

I spend a lot of time seeing and counseling young people who are investigating careers. My advice: be expansive and open to unforeseen opportunities. So many graduates have rigid plans—which I jokingly refer to as their "five-year plans." Often the best things that happen in a person's career development are totally unexpected. Bright people should be more flexible than many seem to be.

# EDUCATION

**M**ANY of the world's most prominent citizens have either started their careers as teachers or have added teaching to the list of their accomplishments. Leonardo da Vinci, Leo Tolstoy, Henry Kissinger, and Jimmy Carter are but a few.

Through the ages the theory of education has fascinated many. Tolstoy put off writing his novels in order to work out his ideas about education, and Plato devoted many of his philosophical treatises to exploring how knowledge is transmitted from teacher to student. People teach, he said, not by writing books or making speeches, but by becoming vitally involved in dialogue, in human relationships. Teaching is something that happens between two people; it is communication, knowledge passing from one to another.

Thousands of years later this still holds true. Ask almost any teacher what constitutes good teaching and he or she will tell you: good teaching is caring for the people you teach. There are less altruistic reasons for becoming a teacher, however, and if you ask a veteran, he or she will probably start with summer vacation—not to mention the three or four weeks of holidays that can accumulate at Christmas, Easter, Thanksgiving, and the scattered celebrations of America's heroes.

Teaching can often serve personal interests, too. For those who love to act, teaching provides the perfect audience. For those who like to be in charge, teaching is one of the few professions where you start off as the boss. For scholars, teaching is a way to delve further into your favorite subjects.

Of course, teaching is not the ideal state. Although the starting salaries can be commensurate with the job market as a whole, salaries for experienced teachers most definitely are not. Crime in the schools has received a lot of national coverage, but what is called crime by the media usually means discipline problems in the school, such as absenteeism, vandalism, and abuse of drugs or alcohol. But prospective teachers must take into account the disciplinary difficulties some of them will encounter.

Perhaps the most troubling problem facing a person interested in a teaching career is the beating teachers' reputations have taken in the last decade. As the quality of education seems to have gone steadily downward, largely because of factors beyond teachers' control, teachers themselves have had to take on more and more responsibilities—not only in the area of teaching, but in the area of genuine care and concern for their students.

Few professions, however, have more social significance than teaching, and none offers the sense of satisfaction that comes from contributing directly and positively to a young person's future. When Wally Schirra, one of the original seven U.S. astronauts, was asked who was the most influential person in his life, he didn't hesitate to say his second-grade teacher.

As computers become standard equipment in more and more classrooms, teacher applicants with computer skills are in a better position to be hired. The educational value of computers, however, depends on how teachers use them. The computer can be used as an automated taskmaster or, more importantly, as an interactive device. Some programs teach sophisticated skills such as thinking and writing even to very small children. Computers can grab and keep a student's attention, stimulate, and motivate him or her to higher levels of achievement. But it is still up to the teacher to provide the crucial interaction that makes learning possible.

# Job Outlook

*Job Openings Will:* Decline

*Competition For Jobs:* Keen

*New Job Opportunities:* If current migration trends continue, a 25% decline in the number of 15 to 19-year-olds is projected in the northeast and north central states between 1980 and 1990. The rate of decline is expected to be 15% in the rest of the country. These statistics, combined with the fact that the 61,650 secondary school teacher applicants from the graduating class of 1981 exceeded the number of job openings by 18,150, indicate that new job opportunities are not plentiful. These statistics do not take into account, however, the graduates who applied for and subsequently accepted positions with independent schools.

Because of the recent budget cuts, school systems have suffered severe cutbacks in expenditures in all areas including teacher hiring and salary increases. But positions do exist, especially in math and computer sciences. Many teachers retire, leave the profession, or find administrative positions, creating thousands of openings each year. Willingness to relocate increases their chances of finding a position.

In 1978 a law was passed mandating special education for all handicapped children. The number of special education teachers rose more than 30 percent between 1970 and 1980, to 187,900. The Department of Education is still predicting a shortage of special ed teachers as the population of children needing special education continues to grow. Job supply is not the only incentive for entering this area; generally, special ed teachers are paid anywhere from $500 to $2000 more per year than other teachers.

Many parents are turning to church-affiliated institutions for the education of their children. Although salaries are almost always lower, job prospects in this area will grow.

New opportunities also exist in the areas of continuing education and preschool education. Adult education courses on virtually every subject imaginable are taught all over the country at local libraries and community centers. The need for nursery schools, some operated by teachers from their own homes, is growing as more and more mothers of young children work full- or part-time.

## Geographic Job Index

The majority of jobs are found in suburban school systems and city schools; fewer positions are available in rural and remote regions. New York, California, Texas, Pennsylvania, Michigan, and Illinois have the greatest teacher populations and the greatest number of new openings for teachers. Since the southwestern and mountain states are growing considerably in population and school enrollments are on the rise, the need for teachers in those areas is growing at a faster rate than anywhere else in the country.

## Who the Employers Are

**PUBLIC SCHOOLS**
Secondary positions: 925,000
Elementary positions: 1,175,000

**PRIVATE SCHOOLS**
Secondary positions: 93,000
Elementary positions: 184,000

California leads the country in the number of private schools with 2444. Of these, 1574 are under the auspices of a religious organization. New York, with 1923, comes in second; 1504 of these schools are church-affiliated.

## How to Break into the Field

Teacher certification requirements vary according to state and are always handled by the state's department of education. The best way to find out how to be certified in a given state is to seek advice from the education department of your college. Many schools of education are members of the National Council of Accreditation of Teacher Education, and graduates of these schools are most likely to be certifiable in every state. Certain education requirements are necessary for teaching in public schools; for teaching in public or most private high schools, you are also required to have majored in the subject in which you wish to teach. Private elementary and high schools usually do not require either certification or education courses.

College placement offices provide the most information and the best service in the quest for a teaching position. Local school systems keep them informed of openings, and more distant job opportunities can be found on their bulletin boards as well. Information can also be found in the classified sections of local newspapers.

An interesting cover letter and résumé addressed to a principal will usually produce a response or an application form. Visiting the community in which you want to find a job can produce contacts and word of mouth recommendations.

Personal recommendations are always a good way to secure a job, particularly in an independent school. Application to an independent school is made to the headmaster through a letter of introduction, and a résumé that should include any extracurricular activities that would make you a more valuable staff member. The best time to apply is in the fall before the year in which you wish to be employed. Hiring decisions are usually made in March or April.

To save time and gather information about out-of-town schools, it can be useful to contact national placement organizations.

Among these are:

North American Educational Consultants
P.O. Box 995
Barre, VT 05641
802-479-0157
(specializes in secondary schools here and abroad)

Careers in Education
P.O. Box 455
East Stroudsburg, PA 18301

Independent Education Services
80 Nassau Street
Princeton, NJ 08540
800-257-5102 (toll free) or 609-921-6195
(specializes in placing prospective private school
        teachers)

Independent Educational Counselors Association
P.O. Box 125
Forest, MA 02644
(specializes in independent schools for the learning
        disabled)

## International Job Opportunities

Opportunities to teach abroad in a variety of subject areas are available to elementary and secondary school teachers through a program sponsored by the United States Information Agency. An applicant must have at least a bachelor's degree, be a United States citizen, and have three years of successful full-time teaching experience, preferably in the subject and at the level for which an application is made. Information and application materials may be obtained from:

Teacher Exchange Branch
United States Information Agency
301 Fourth Street, S.W.
Washington, DC 20547

Opportunities to teach abroad aren't limited to those with three years of teaching experience. For example, speaking Russian can lead you to be sponsored by the American Field Service to participate in an exchange program with the Soviet Union. The Peace Corps, the National Education Association, and UNESCO all offer opportunities for teachers abroad. The most comprehensive brochure on the subject, *Study and Teaching Opportunities Abroad* by Pat Kern McIntyre, can be obtained from the U.S. Department of Education, Washington, DC 20402.

# TEACHING

## Qualifications

*Personal:* A genuine desire to work with and care for young people. Ability to lead a group. Strong character. Stamina. Creativity. Well organized.

*Professional:* College degree. For public schools, certification as well. High school teachers are usually required to have majored in the subject they choose to teach. For elementary school teaching you need a broad range of knowledge and interests, including some instinct for children and how they develop.

## Career Paths

| LEVEL | JOB TITLE | EXPERIENCE NEEDED |
|-------|-----------|-------------------|
| Entry | Teacher | College degree; certification as required |
| 1 | Teacher (with master's) | Master's degree in education or in subject area |
| 3 | Department Head (high school) | 7-10 years |

## Job Responsibilities

## Entry Level

THE BASICS:   Presenting subject matter. Developing lesson plans. Preparing and giving examinations. Arranging class and individual projects that contribute to the learning process. Attending parent conferences, field trips, and faculty meetings. In junior and senior high schools, homeroom guidance, study hall supervision.

MORE CHALLENGING DUTIES:   Club leadership. Sports coach or leading support for sports activities. Directing activities in which the entire school participates, such as assemblies or fund raisers.

## Moving Up

Opportunities for advancement exist in the field of education, especially for those with energy, ideas, and the ability to communicate with both adults and children. Administrators, principals, and superintendents can earn up to $45,000 per year and have a major influence on the communities they serve. To move into administrative or supervisory positions, you must have one year of graduate education, several years of classroom experience, and sometimes a special certificate, depending on the state.

The concept of master teacher is a new one, but school systems in Texas are already awarding teachers who achieve this level—by virtue of experience and effectiveness—with greater responsibility, status and a significant increase in pay. High school teachers have the opportunity to become department heads.

Good and creative teachers with some years of experience are in an excellent position to become educational consultants either as editors of textbooks, directors of special programs, or within the school system as curriculum developers. Especially in the areas of math and the sciences, experienced teachers are being pulled from the classroom to teach other teachers.

To move up in the field of education, you have to have the ability to deal with all kinds of people in all kinds of sensitive situations.

You must have a dedication to the job that continues long after school's over. And you must show a willingness to continue your own education, gaining a master's degree or even a doctoral degree in education or in your subject area.

Teaching can also be a springboard into other professions. Businesses have long known that the experience one gets as a teacher is excellent training for executive positions in marketing, public relations, and advertising. The analytical skills that teachers develop in the classroom, as well as the ability to deal with many different people at many different levels, cannot be taught in a business school. These skills that teachers use day in and day out can be effectively transferred to the business world.

## ADDITIONAL INFORMATION

### Salaries

Teachers progress in salary as they gain experience. Salaries vary widely from state to state. Starting annual salaries can range from $10,000 to $16,000, but generally higher salaries are to be found in the suburban areas. According to the National Educational Association, for secondary and elementary teachers, in 1982-83, the state with the highest average annual salary was Alaska at $33,953. Washington, DC, came in second with an average salary of $26,045. The lowest paying states were Mississippi, with $14,285; Arkansas, with $15,176; and Vermont, with $15,338.

The salary of an independent secondary school teacher is not commensurate with that of a public school teacher, although there are fringe benefits that can often compensate for the difference in pay. At boarding schools, teachers can expect to receive free room and board or rent-reduced housing on or near campus. Travel expenses and smaller workloads also help to compensate for smaller salaries.

## Working Conditions

*Hours:*   Most teachers spend between six and seven hours a day with 15 to 30 children, but that is far from the end of the day. Experienced teachers can often get by with a quick review of their old lesson plans, but new teachers should anticipate an extra two or three hours a day for preparation and correction. Some of the work can be done during the summer vacation and the three or four weeks of holiday during the year.

*Environment:*   This can range from the rolling hills of a rural boarding school to the bleak insides of an inner-city school. Teachers can have access to tennis courts, swimming pools, even a stable full of horses, or they may have to content themselves, for recreation, with the smoke-filled faculty room.

The classroom environment is generally what you make it. Elementary teachers can plaster their walls with children's art, waxed leaves in fall, cutouts of flowers in spring. In secondary schools, decoration can be anything from a chart of chemical elements to a poster of the rock star of the moment.

*Workstyle:*   Most classrooms consist of a blackboard, a big desk, and 20 or 30 smaller ones facing front. Yet each teacher has the choice to make each class either student-centered or teacher-centered. Some teachers prefer to lecture or read to their students; other promote student discussion to various degrees. History teachers have discovered that role-playing and mini-dramas can give life to an epoch. English classes can concentrate on grammar, literature, or writing. With the availability of computers, students are less likely to tune out of math class because of the possibilities for direct interaction and feedback. The art room can offer the freest environment. Many teachers turn on music while students paint or sculpt, and students chat among themselves or with the teacher as they work. The major environmental factor in any class will always be the moods and attitudes of the students, and this is where the good teacher becomes the chief architect of his or her surroundings.

*Travel:* If travel is your end, teaching abroad can be your means. Class trips and outings are also available to the enterprising teacher. Schools will often pay the expenses of a teacher attending a conference, chaperoning a team to an out-of-town match, or accompanying students to recreational activities.

## Extracurricular Activities/Work Experience

Volunteer—Big Brother/Sister program, tutoring, sports, summer camps, teen counseling, child care centers for retarded or culturally disadvantaged children

Athletics—sports (participation can lead to coaching positions in secondary schools)

School—cheerleading, debate society, literary clubs, student newspapers, yearbook publications, student government, drama club, glee club, art club, alumni/admissions administrative work

## Internships

Aside from the student teaching that accompanies college or graduate certification and degree programs, there are few opportunities for teaching internships, except at a limited number of independent schools. They offer the opportunity to get experience in teaching without taking on the responsibility of a full-time teacher. Under the tutelage of a head teacher, the intern learns the ins and outs of the profession. Both school and intern benefit from such a program and the intern is often paid a nominal salary. Contact individual independent schools to see if they have a program.

## Recommended Reading

**BOOKS**

*Don't Smile Until Christmas: Accounts of the First Year of Teaching,* Kevin Ryan, ed. University of Chicago Press: 1970

*The Teacher Rebellion* by David Selden, Howard University Press: 1970

*Teaching School: Points Picked Up* by Eric Johnson, Walker & Company: 1979

**PERIODICALS**

*Academic Journal: The Educator's Employment Magazine* (biweekly), Box 392, Newton, CT 06470

*American Education* (ten times a year), U.S. Department of Education, 400 Maryland Avenue, S.W., Washington, DC 20202

*Arithmetic Teacher/Mathematics Teacher* (ten times a year), 11906 Association Drive, Reston, VA 22091

*The Association for School, College and University (ASCUS) Staffing Annual: A Job Search Handbook for Educators* (annual), Box 411, Madison, WI 53711

*Chronicle of Higher Education* (weekly), 1333 New Hampshire Avenue, N.W., Washington, DC 20036

*Harvard Educational Review* (quarterly), Graduate School of Education, Harvard University, 13 Appian Way, Cambridge, MA 02138

*Today's Education* (quarterly), National Education Association, 1201 Sixteenth Street, N.W., Washington, DC 20036

## Professional Associations

American Federation of Teachers
11 Dupont Circle, N.W.
Washington, DC 20036

Association for School, College and University Staffing
ASCUS Office
Box 411
Madison, WI 53711

National Education Association
1201 Sixteenth Street, N.W.
Washington, DC 20036

# INTERVIEWS

**Margaret Thompson, Age 39**
**Secondary School Teacher**
**Needham High School and Newman Middle School, Needham, MA**

Although the competition for English teaching positions is very fierce now, in five or ten years there should be a real market. If you're lucky enough to find a position right now, though, it can be the most rewarding experience of your life.

There's autonomy. You're your own boss. Once you're in that classroom, the door is shut. You can be amazingly creative. Every single day is a new challenge. And you get to show off a lot. Probably more than any other subject, teaching English calls on you to perform.

Teaching English is like conducting an orchestra. You're in charge, but the students have to play their own instruments. The more they play their instruments, the happier they are. And when they can hear those instruments being played together in an orchestra it gives them a big thrill.

For example, sixth and seventh graders are being introduced to literature for the first time in their lives; you teach them about the components of a story—the climax, the development, the resolution; then they read the story and for the first time have a sense of recognition; they're reading about characters who are experiencing some of the same conflicts they are. They listen to each other's interpretations and all of a sudden they don't feel alone anymore.

I think literature is one of the most subtle ways of affecting people's lives. You have to know how to choose the literature that will be the catalyst to self-understanding and give students the structural tools to explore their own lives.

What kind of person would really have fun teaching? A caring person. One who enjoys stroking and being stroked. I've been teaching for 13 years now. I'm making about maximum salary, $26,000 a year. But the feeling of loving more than balances the salary. I'll never stop teaching. It's a joy.


**Laura Daigen, Age 29**
**Fourth-Grade Teacher**
**New York, NY**


I started out teaching Spanish in a high school, but I decided there was a lot more good to be done as a bilingual elementary teacher. I was somewhat disillusioned with the politics of the school where I worked. Teachers who had been there longer made sure that they had no problem students in their classes and that kids with low test scores were taught by the rookies. The Spanish language textbooks were poor and antiquated in their absence of girls and women.

When you're working in a public school in the inner city, the needs of your kids are infinite. There's very little support from the administration or cohesiveness among the faculty. You're alone with kids who have more emotional needs than you can deal with. There is no one to help you help them.

Even under the best of conditions, the hours are long. Sometimes I'm there until six or seven and I'm not the last one to leave. I'm making plans for new curriculum, I'm marking papers, I'm cleaning up the room. You're never finished when you're a teacher: you dream it, you go to sleep thinking about it, and you wake up thinking about it. You're teaching eleven pieces of curriculum and you have to coordinate them and give enough time to each one. It was easier teaching Spanish in a high school, because I was teaching one subject at three different levels and the students had the responsibility of absorbing what you gave them. But when you're teaching elementary school and the kid isn't learning, it's your fault.

If someone were trying to decide whether or not to go into teaching, the first question I would ask him or her is: Do you like kids? Are you ready to take on the responsibility of little human beings and their emotional needs? There is tremendous satisfaction in watching children grow, seeing them move out of themselves and being able to give; recognizing their right to receive fair treatment knowing they can effect change if they see an injustice being done. It feels great to have a kid say, "I like math this year," or "I don't have to try to read these books, I can just read them," or to see kids take charge of their own lives and take pride in what they've done on their own.

I think what makes a good teacher is the sincerity of his or her commitment—whatever it is. It can be to help children love reading or to help them see themselves as important pieces of society or to help them realize the value of their own ethnicity. It has to be more than a vague "I love kids"—but you have to love kids, too.

No matter what I end up doing with my life, I'll always be able to look back on these five or six years and say those were years that I spent doing what I really wanted to do. Perhaps I haven't been well-compensated economically, but the job is rewarding. I will always be able to say that I did something that was meaningful, something that helped others.

---
✳
---

# GOVERNMENT

S ETTING aside any judgment on the controversy about the size of government—is it too big, or not big enough?—the simple fact is that today government is the single largest employer in the United States. Millions work for federal, state, and local governments in an endless variety of jobs. Virtually every profession and trade found in the private and nonprofit sectors are found in the public sector. Whatever your skills and interests, and whatever profession you have chosen to pursue, a place may be waiting for you in government service.

For many people, government is more than an employer, it is a career choice in itself. They find government service appealing because they know that their efforts contribute to the nation, the state, or the community. On the less idealistic side, many government jobs, particularly those at the federal level, offer excellent opportunities for on-the-job training. Often, you can move quickly into a management position. Government also offers exceptional benefits and job security.

The skills of the political science or government major are obviously geared to government service. Political scientists are employed to conduct research and analysis in the areas of public policy and public administration, and some work in the legal system. However, graduate degrees are almost invariably required; the comparatively few entry-level positions open to those with only a bachelor's degree demand a superior academic record and a background of extensive research.

Government also provides a number of other unique personal and career opportunities not found elsewhere. Three opportunities with the federal government that should be of special interest to the political science major are:

- **The Peace Corps**
- **Intelligence Services**
- **Foreign Service**

If you are intrigued by any of these, begin your investigation early in your academic career. Each is highly selective and requires specific skills and experience. You must be well-prepared by the time you graduate in order to compete.

## Job Outlook

*Job Openings Will Grow:*   More slowly than average

*Competition for Jobs:*   Keen
Government hiring policies at the local, state, and federal levels are affected by political decisions. By decree or legislative action, a new department, agency, or bureau may be created, an established organization eliminated, or existing offices merged. Since 1980, a strong movement against big government has produced hiring freezes throughout the federal government. The greatest need is for individuals with advanced degrees (computer science, biology, health, and agricultural specialties, among others) and in clerical positions. Neither option is suited for those with undergraduate degrees. White-collar entry-level job openings

are limited or nonexistent in most departments (the Department of Defense is a notable exception, but even it is not hiring extensively). Although attitudes and politics may change, the simple fact remains that there is a glut of federal employees. To ease the situation, the jobs of many individuals who leave government service are not being refilled.

But as job opportunities dwindle at the federal level, they are growing at the state and local levels. As Washington, DC, requires these governmental bodies to provide services once handled by federal agencies, administrative and managerial positions are being created.

## Geographic Job Index

The Washington, DC, metropolitan area has the highest concentration of federal jobs. Most federal departments and agencies are headquartered either in the city itself or in the Virginia-Maryland suburbs. However, federal offices are spread across the United States. Some offices, such as the Internal Revenue Service and the Federal Bureau of Investigation, are found in every state; others, such as the State Department and the National Archives, have branches in key cities. Military installations often create high numbers of nonmilitary jobs in the areas around them. When applying to the federal government, relocation is an important consideration. Your willingness to move may increase your chances of winning a coveted position.

At the state and local levels, you will find the highest concentrations of jobs in state capitals, county seats and large cities.

## How to Break into the Field

Unlike many other employers, the federal government offers a great deal of aid to job-hunters, but because you are dealing with a bureaucracy, red-tape hassles are unavoidable. Be prepared to be aggressive, assertive, and, above all, patient in your job search.

The place to begin is a federal job information office (check the Yellow Pages for the nearest location). Here you can learn about the various jobs within the federal government, as well as the current hiring outlook. The information centers have publications called occupational briefs, each of which describes a job in detail. These brochures are also available at libraries, but only at an information center are you sure to get the most recent information.

You should first determine if the position you seek is within the competitive service or the excepted service. Jobs in the competitive service are handled through the federal government's central personnel agency, the Office of Personnel Management. Departments and agencies that hire under the excepted service have their own personnel departments. In either case, you file a basic application called Standard Form 171 and submit an academic transcript. Some departments require additional procedures—written tests, security checks, medical exams, and others. Your qualifications are evaluated and you are given a numerical rating and placed on a register. When your name appears at the top of the register, your application is submitted to offices that are hiring. If you have not noted any geographic restrictions, you could be considered by any potential federal employer anywhere in the country. You may be interviewed in person or, if the office is distant, over the phone.

An application may be renewed each year by reporting all pertinent work experience. Although work experience can give you an edge over other candidates, a career in government should be started within a few years after graduation. The federal government prefers to promote from within. An outside (or "non-status") person will be hired for a management position instead of a government ("status") employee only if the position requires very specific skills.

There are U.S. Government Offices of Personnel Management in Washington, DC, Atlanta, GA, Boston, MA, Chicago, IL, Dallas, TX, Denver, CO, New York, NY, Philadelphia, PA, St. Louis, MO, San Francisco, CA, and Seattle, WA.

State and local governments also have personnel departments. The hiring process may be similar to that of the federal government, but should be less complicated.

Again, the first step is to find out where job information is available and to whom applications must be addressed. Many state and local governments require that their employees reside in the political division, which could be an important consideration in your job search.

## International Job Opportunities

In addition to obvious international jobs, such as the foreign service and the Peace Corps, the federal government offers a number of opportunities to work abroad. The Office of Personnel Management and Federal Job Information Centers have information on the types of overseas jobs available and the qualifications. In many instances, competence in a foreign language is preferred or required. (Keep in mind that a large number of these international opportunities are for clerical personnel.)

# THE PEACE CORPS

More than 5000 Americans work as Peace Corps volunteers in the developing nations of Africa, Asia, Latin America and the Pacific. They work on an endless variety of projects—starting a chicken farm, building a road system, working in hospitals or with youth. Americans of any age and background can apply, and many are recent college graduates. All offer their skills as volunteers, making two-year commitments, and serve as guests of the host countries. You may work on projects funded by the United States government, or you may receive funds from other governments or international agencies. You may work with other volunteers—either from the Peace Corps or from other organizations, including non-American ones—or you may be sent on an assignment alone.

Service in the Peace Corps does not mark the beginning of a set career path. Some former volunteers work as administrators with the Peace Corps, but no one serves with this purpose in mind.

Instead, individuals apply because of the extraordinary experiences offered. Your courage, endurance, and creativity and your managerial, organizational, and interpersonal skills are tested in situations completely unlike any you have known. You become a friend, teacher, and partner to the people you work with, adapting to their culture and living in the same surroundings. You may find yourself in an isolated mountain village or on a remote South Sea island, surrounded by people who have had limited exposure to Americans. You may have to contend with some resentment to outside intrusion, and you risk your personal safety by living with primitive sanitation and health facilities.

Although the personal rewards should be your primary concern, Peace Corps experience can be a valuable asset if you plan a career in the international sector, whether that career is the foreign service, the United Nations (although opportunities for United States citizens are extremely limited there) or other international organizations, or in international business. It is equally valuable if you plan to teach, do research, or write about global affairs. The experience can also enhance advanced studies in Third World politics, international relations, or global economics.

Applicants are carefully screened by former volunteers. Good intentions are not enough; you should be able to demonstrate some skills in agriculture, construction, nutrition, business, science, or health and community service. Volunteers receive 8 to 12 weeks of training in the United States, which can include a crash course in native language and customs. Usually, volunteers are sent to host countries in groups; however, chances are good that once you arrive you will not be working with other volunteers. You may start a project from scratch, or work in established institutions, such as schools and hospitals.

During your two-year commitment, you receive a modest living allowance, transportation to and from your assignment, and a small compensation (presently $175 per month) that is given you on your return.

For application information, write:

The Peace Corps
806 Connecticut Avenue, N.W.
Washington, DC 20526

# INTELLIGENCE SERVICES

The cloak-and-dagger intrigues of spying have given way to satellite photography and reams of computer-generated statistics. The secret agent still serves a purpose, but twentieth-century intelligence gathering has evolved from Mata Hari to modern science. The federal government employs large staffs of skilled people with varied backgrounds, all of whom endeavor to analyze and understand the current world situation.

The two main sources of intelligence gathering for the United States government are the Central Intelligence Agency (CIA) and the less well-known Defense Intelligence Agency (DIA). The CIA reports directly to the president and the National Security Council, providing information on the world situation as it relates to national security. The DIA also investigates international matters, but is responsible for providing information directly to the Department of Defense. Although it serves the military, DIA analysts are nonmilitary personnel. In many respects, both organizations analyze the same data, but the users of this information and their purposes in requesting it are different.

The DIA closely monitors foreign military affairs. The agency assesses the strength and preparedness of foreign armed forces, the types and quantities of their equipment, the movement of these forces and the new weapons they develop. To complement its understanding of military affairs, the DIA investigates the history, politics, economics, geography, industrial capability, and resources of a nation. This agency keeps up-to-date information on foreign military installations, tracks compliance with international arms agreements, and will, if necessary, investigate the status of prisoners of war and answer questions about those missing in action.

The DIA has also become concerned with watching the growth and activities of international terrorist organizations. The information gathered about these groups is vital to the safety of American military and foreign service personnel.

The CIA monitors these same areas, but its efforts are not focused on foreign military affairs. This organization is more concerned with the political and social situations in other countries. It does not make decisions on how the United States government should react to international events, but provides information to those officials who do set national policy.

The job of the intelligence analyst in either agency is to gather all bits of information, which may be fragmentary or secondhand, and to try to create a coherent image of a nation or a particular international problem.

The political scientist is needed to analyze the political, historical, cultural, and social institutions of a nation. You seek to understand the political parties, the dominant personalities and the other forces that shape government structures.

In many jobs the ability to speak or read a foreign language is a valuable asset. For example, the CIA has an entire department devoted simply to following international news media. Both agencies offer opportunities to work abroad for a part of your career, but options are available only to experienced personnel.

Both agencies hire outside the Office of Personnel Management. Each subjects applicants to medical exams and stringent security checks. Many applicants have advanced degrees, but those with bachelor's degrees are considered. Each agency has an extensive training program for entry-level personnel.

At the entry level, you are responsible for gathering information from various sources. The more advanced you become, the more you will be involved in analysis. Continuing education is an important part of any intelligence career. Your agency will offer classes that will increase your knowledge and expertise, and you may be required to study at a university or college.

For information on careers in the CIA, write:

Director of Personnel
Central Intelligence Agency
Washington, DC 20505

For information on careers with the DIA, write:

Defense Intelligence Agency
Civilian Personnel Operation Division
Recruitment Office
Washington, DC 20301

# FOREIGN SERVICE

The foreign service serves the President and the Secretary of State by planning and conducting United States foreign policy. Foreign Service officers (FSO) work at the State Department in Washington, DC, and in over 230 embassies, missions, and consulates around the world. The foreign service offers an unusually varied career, but the decision to explore this department should not be taken lightly. You will be successful and happy only if you have extraordinary discipline and commitment, and view the benefits as far outweighing the sacrifices.

The foreign service is among the most competitive careers you might explore. Simply getting an offer of a foreign service commission is difficult; throughout a life of service, you can expect to compete against other skilled FSOs for virtually every assignment and promotion.

Obviously, only United States citizens are eligible. You must first sit for the foreign service exam, offered the first Saturday of each December. A broad knowledge of domestic and foreign affairs, with an emphasis on American history, government and culture, is required. English skills are tested, because an FSO must articulate United States policies. A test of specific skill areas determines the elements of foreign service work best suited to your abilities.

If you pass the test, you are given an all-day oral assessment of your background, temperament, and attitudes. Finally, you must pass a medical exam. With these requirements successfully completed, you are placed on one or more registers, depending on your skills and interests. Each register leads to placement in one of five functional areas: political, economic, administrative, consular, and informational-cultural. The number of openings varies from year to year, but of the approximately 12,000 people who take the test each December, perhaps 300 will eventually be commissioned. The majority of appointees have advanced degrees or work experience or both; their maturity and increased knowledge make the competition even tougher for recent graduates.

If you are accepted into the foreign service, you are given several weeks of orientation at the Foreign Service Institute, followed by up to seven months of training. Fluency in a foreign language is not a requirement for application, but it is an asset. FSOs are instructed in a language, and the length of your training is largely determined by your needs in this area. Your career prospects are enhanced by competence in several languages. The foreign service is particularly interested in applicants who speak Russian, Arabic, Mandarin Chinese, and other languages rarely studied by Americans.

Sixty percent of the average FSO career is spent abroad, and an important prerequisite for application is a willingness to be assigned anywhere. You may be pleased at the thought of working in Hong Kong or Brussels, but how do you feel about Ouagadougou, Port Moresby, and Tegucigalpa? In many parts of the world, respect for diplomatic immunity can no longer be taken for granted, and the threat of international terrorism is forcing embassies to adopt once-unimagined security measures. Personal safety has become an important consideration, especially for officers with families. Regardless of the capacity in which you serve, the most important part of your job is defending and winning support for United States policies, even those contrary to your personal opinions.

There are five principal areas in which you may serve.

Political Affairs:   As a political officer, you analyze the political situation in the country to which you are posted, and present United States policies to officials of that nation's government. In Washington, DC, political officers serve in State Department offices that specialize in various regions. They analyze embassy reports, brief government officials, and work with foreign diplomats accredited to Washington.

Economic Affairs:   Economic officers stationed abroad interpret United States economic policies while analyzing and reporting on foreign economies. To understand a nation's economy, the officer studies local finances, trade, resources, and industries. In Washington, DC, economic officers contribute to the formulation of national and international economic policies.

If you do well in the economic portion of the foreign service exam, you may also be considered for appointment to the Foreign Commercial Service. Here you work under the direction of the Department of Commerce rather than the Department of State. The Foreign Commercial Service Officer is stationed abroad and seeks to promote trade between the United States and a foreign nation. The job involves a great deal of work with local business and government officials, so language skills are extremely important.

Administrative Affairs:   Overseas, administrative officers are concerned with daily operations of embassies and consulates, such as personnel, budgeting, security, and communications. In Washington, DC, they provide support for those stationed abroad.

Consular Services:   Here you work closely with the public, both American citizens and foreign nationals, by dealing with passport, visa, and immigration concerns. Foreign language skills are extremely important. Consular officers are stationed in embassies and consulates, which are located in key foreign cities. In Washington, DC, the Bureau of Consular Affairs provides support for consular officers abroad with guidance and aid in problem situations.

United States International Communication Agency:   This agency strives to give foreign people an understanding of American culture, attitudes, institutions, and values. Service as a foreign service information officer means getting to know a foreign society while explaining our own by importing and disseminating American art, films, and journalism. You might also be involved in organizing educational and cultural exchange programs. An important part of your job will be to invite American lecturers, performers, and athletes to visit the country in which you are stationed. Information officers in Washington help to coordinate these visits.

## Career Paths

Your career path will vary with the changing policies and needs of the State Department. You are reassigned at intervals of two to four years, often alternating an overseas posting with a stay in Washington, DC. However, assignments are entirely dependent on your skills and where they can best be used at any given time. Experienced FSOs are expected to specialize in a function, such as political affairs or consular services. However, in practice, most FSOs perform a variety of jobs. Officers are ranked, and promotions depend on annual ratings.

An ambassadorship is publicly perceived as the highest foreign service post. However, in reality, most United States ambassadors are political appointees who have little or no foreign service experience. Some skilled FSOs reach the level of senior foreign service officers. These may be appointed as ambassadors, but most senior officers remain in the United States, guiding State Department policies and programs.

For information on foreign service careers, write:

Foreign Service Management
Officer Recruitment Branch
P.O. Box 9317
Rosslyn Station
Arlington, VA 22209

# ADDITIONAL INFORMATION

## Salaries

Although governmental bodies often pay their employees less than private industries, they offer attractive perks. Government employees receive generous vacation and sick leave, exceptional benefits, and pension and early retirement plans.

Most federal employees, including the CIA and the DIA are paid according to a standard pay schedule. Each promotion is accompanied by a change of GS rating. The typical graduate is hired as a GS-5 or GS-7, depending on academic record and work experience. A graduate degree holder is hired at GS-9. In the foreign service, the pay schedule is comparable to that in other government jobs, but varies according to the nation in which you are stationed. Foreign Service Officers in many countries receive hardship pay and/or living allowances.

The following chart gives the federal white-collar annual pay schedule as of January 1, 1984 (figures are the lowest wages for each GS rating).

| GS1 | $ 8,980 | GS10 | $23,088 |
|-----|---------|------|---------|
| GS2 | $10,097 | GS11 | $25,366 |
| GS3 | $11,017 | GS12 | $30,402 |
| GS4 | $12,367 | GS13 | $36,152 |
| GS5 | $13,837 | GS14 | $42,722 |
| GS6 | $15,423 | GS15 | $50,252 |
| GS7 | $17,138 | GS16 | $58,938 |
| GS8 | $18,981 | GS17 | $69,042 |
| GS9 | $20,965 | GS18 | $80,920 |

## Extracurricular Activities/Work Experience

Model United Nations
Student Government
Participation in a language house or organizations that
    investigate other cultures
Writing for campus publications, particularly those that
    deal with national and international affairs

## Internships

The federal government sponsors an excellent program of cooperative education for undergraduates. However, for you to be eligible, your college must participate in the program.

Students from a wide variety of majors are recruited to work full-time or part-time at a government agency. Most positions are for those with a specific academic concentration, such as accounting and computer science. Students with other backgrounds can find openings, but opportunities are more limited. For information, consult your school's internship or placement office.

The Department of State offers plenty of options for students interested in a foreign service career. You may be a summer intern, which is a paying position, or you may intern during a fall or spring semester, which is not compensated. Applications for a summer position must be submitted by the preceding November 1; applications for a fall or spring internship must be received at least six months in advance. Students must be juniors or seniors, have studied some pertinent coursework, and be willing to permit a background investigation before they are accepted.

For information, write:

Intern Coordinator
Department of State
P.O. Box 9317
Rosslyn Station
Arlington, VA 22209-0317

## Recommended Reading

**BOOKS**

*American Foreign Policy* by Henry Kissinger, W.W. Norton: 1977

*Caveat: Realism, Reagan and Foreign Policy* by Alexander Haig, Macmillan Publishing Company: 1984

*Dictatorships and Double Standards: Rationalism and Realism in Politics* by Jeanne Kirkpatrick, Simon and Schuster: 1982

*Hard Choices: Four Critical Years in Managing America's Foreign Policy* by Cyrus Vance, Simon and Schuster: 1983

*World Almanac Book of Facts,* World Almanac: 1984

**PERIODICALS**

*Department of State Bulletin* (monthly), United States Department of State, Washington, DC 20520

*Development Digest* (quarterly), United States Department of State, Agency for International Development, United States Government Printing Office, Superintendent of Documents, Washington, DC 20402

*Foreign Affairs* (bimonthly), 58 East 68th Street, New York, NY 10021

*Foreign Service Journal* (weekly), Foreign Service Association, 2101 E Street, N.W., Washington, DC 20037

*Government Employee Relations Report* (weekly), The Bureau of National Affairs, 1231 25th Street, Washington, DC 20037

*State* (monthly), United States Department of State, United States Government Printing Office, Superintendent of Documents, Washington, DC 20402

## Professional Associations

American Council of Voluntary Agencies for Foreign
    Service
200 Park Avenue South
New York, NY 10003

American Foreign Policy Institute
1101 17th Street, N.W.
Suite 1000
Washington, DC 20036

National Committee on American Foreign Policy
200 Park Avenue
Suite 4416
New York, NY 10017

# INTERVIEWS

**Edwin Jorge**
**Recruiter and Former Volunteer**
**Peace Corps, New York, NY**

Before I joined the Peace Corps, I had worked my way up to vice president of a nonprofit organization that dealt with economic development for minorities. I had been aware of the Peace Corps since its inception, and in 1979 I decided that I was financially secure enough to leave my job and become a volunteer.

Because I was born in the Caribbean, I wanted to be posted to that part of the world. I was sent to Jamaica as a community development specialist. I went with the intention of doing something to help the children of Jamaica. I started off with $2000 in seed money from the Canadian government and with it I started programs to get delinquent boys off the streets. We taught them math and English and eventually started a vocational program in auto mechanics. The Street Corner Boys' Program, as it was called, grew to include a medical and dental program and, finally, a hot lunch program. In addition to the Canadian donation, I received funds from the Dutch government and some Norwegian expatriates, and the assistance of Mitzi Seaga, the wife of the prime minister. By the time I left Kingston, that initial $2000 had grown to a total operating budget of over $150,000, including gifts-in-kind. I enjoyed my work and was satisfied that I had accomplished a lot of what I had set out to do. As far as I know, these programs are still operating.

When I finished my two years, I knew I wanted to stay with the Peace Corps and that I wanted to recruit. I felt I had a good idea of what makes a good volunteer, and I wanted to contribute to the Corps by ensuring that only the best people are sent abroad. Because of what I had accomplished in Kingston, I was given an excellent recommendation and moved directly into recruiting.

I interview candidates and decide if they have what it takes to be volunteers. A recruiter has to be an excellent judge of character, because there is no lack of applicants. Each candidate is assigned to a recruiter. If I get someone who is well-qualified, it is my responsibility to get that person to make a commitment and volunteer.

We are especially interested in finding people who have been involved in the community. We also like to see some demonstrated interest in the Third World, but that is not an absolute requirement. The key to being accepted is proving that you want to work with people and that you will be able to live in another culture.

To be quite honest, the Peace Corps is the best job I've ever had. I love it. When I made the decision to become a recruiter, I took a cut in salary that left me with half of what I was making when I went into the Corps as a volunteer. I wouldn't change that decision for anything.

**Stephanie Smith Kinney, Age 40**
**Foreign Service Officer; Uruguay/Paraguay Desk, Bureau**
        **of Inter-American Affairs**
**Department of State, Washington, DC**

My interest in the foreign service goes back a long way. I first investigated it in high school and my research had discouraging results. At that time, I discovered, a foreign service career was difficult for women. Female officers did not go beyond mid-level positions, married women weren't accepted, and if a female officer married, an unwritten rule compelled her to resign.

But I kept my long-standing interest in the rest of the world. At Vassar, I majored in Spanish literature and Latin American affairs.

I spent my junior year at the University of Madrid. I was interested in teaching, so I went on for a master's in education at Harvard.

The foreign service reentered my life when my husband became a foreign service officer about a year after we were married. His first assignment was Mexico City, which he accepted at my instigation. I wanted to be in a Spanish-speaking country because I thought I could use my background. I experienced the difficulty of being a foreign service spouse when I found that restrictions prevented me from working. I fought the regulations and became the first United States foreign service spouse officially permitted to work in Mexico City.

When we returned to Washington in 1974 we were faced with a choice: sacrifice my desire for a career, my husband's career, or our marriage. I decided the easiest option was to try to change the system in which my husband worked. I became part of a group that was working to get the State Department to be more concerned with the problems of foreign service spouses and families.

I finally decided that the best way to fight the foreign service was to join it (married women were no longer excluded), and I passed the exam and the orals and was accepted as an officer in 1976. One of my first assignments was as a management analyst charged with looking into family issues and "solving the growing spouse problems." I was a key force in creating the Family Liaison Office, the headquarters of which was inaugurated in the State Department in March 1977. Today, it has 92 branches overseas, which help family members deal with the myriad problems posed by their highly mobile, international life-style.

From that start I've done a variety of things. I'm in the administrative function or "cone," but I've never had a truly administrative job. Now I'm on a political desk, Uruguay and Paraguay. Before that, I was with the United States Information Agency in New York. I served as assistant science attaché and also did consular and press work in Rome, and I worked in cultural affairs for West Africa in the Department.

The best and the most successful people rarely conform to structure—if you're creative, you cut your own path. My own career has been a combination of coincidence and necessity. My husband and I try to coordinate our assignments, but we must always apply individually. If a couple is not given assignments at the same post, they may take separate assignments or one spouse may take leave without pay.

If you are considering a career in the foreign service, you must be a generalist: have a background in American culture and history, economics, public administration, and political analysis. You should be confident that you can learn a foreign language. Some experience abroad is an asset—if only because it proves you can work in another culture. You must have a sense of conviction about the United States—a sense of what we are and what we should be—and a willingness to serve it. On the personal side, you must have social graces (or a willingness to learn them), a high tolerance for frustration, a sense of adventure, optimism, and a sense of humor. Although you play a defined role in a tradition-bound profession, what enables you to perform is your own sense of purpose.

It is important that you think through your priorities and your needs as a person. What do you want in a career? Do you want marriage? Children? It is difficult enough to combine a family and a career when you stay in one place—it's that much more difficult in a highly mobile career. People often see only the glamour and excitement of foreign service life—to the exclusion of the drudgery, danger, and sacrifice it can also require. It's not just a job, it's a total commitment—so it's better not to approach it with any illusions.

# LAW

T HE practice of law offers a wide variety of career choices for liberal arts graduates. The long arm of the law is an apt phrase not only to describe the law's ability to deal with its violators, but also to point to the fact that the law touches each and every one of us in our daily lives. Few transactions in our complex society— even common ones such as the purchase of a home or a share of stock—are not subject to laws and regulations; skilled interpreters of these laws are in great demand. And everyday lawyer advocates in our nations's civil and criminal courts argue to protect the rights of society and of individuals, and address the fundamental questions of what is fair and just.

The research, writing, and analytical skills of the liberal arts graduate are particularly well-suited to the study and practice of law. Much of a lawyer's work entails reading documents, and then preparing a written presentation of the findings. (For those with a flair for the dramatic, the law also offers the opportunity to argue a case orally in a court.) In its essence this process is one that an English major will find familiar from reading and interpreting poems and novels; the history major will recognize the process from examining and drawing conclusions from historical documents and evidence; the political science major will draw similar parallels from the study of political trends and philosophy.

The majority of lawyers work in one of the following three areas: corporate practice, government service, or private practice. A chapter of this size can only provide the barest outlines of the opportunities available to aspiring lawyers. For this reason an entire book in this series—*Career Choices for Undergraduates Considering Law*—has been devoted to the practice of law.

## Job Outlook

*Job Openings Will Grow:*   About as fast as average

*Competition for Jobs:*   Strong to keen

*New Job Opportunities:*   Generally speaking, the outlook for job opportunities with corporations is excellent. Corporations have traditionally depended on private corporate law firms to handle their legal affairs. In recent years, however, many corporations are depending more heavily, and often completely, on inside counsel. The reasons for this trend are largely economic; fees charged by private firms have become so high that most corporations feel they can save money by having their own attorneys on their payroll. Although there will be fluctuations in specific industries caused by economic trends and any other events that would influence business, the general outlook should still remain favorable.

With budget restraints and the current trend toward deregulation and decentralization, there are few growth areas in government service. On the federal side, immigration law is assuming a new importance; on the state and local side, there is a need to take up the slack created by the loosening of federal controls and the decrease in federal services.

Demand for private practitioners rises and falls with national and local shifts in politics and the hot areas in law practice today are mergers and acquisitions, bankruptcy, real estate, and tax, while decreased governmental regulation has lessened the demand for lawyers in such areas as labor law, environmental law, and antitrust. Rapid-fire technological advances—in areas ranging from telecommunications to new life forms—have opened up a new world of job opportunities for lawyers with backgrounds in science and engineering.

Also look for increased job opportunities in areas involving alternatives to litigation as a means of resolving disputes. Current trends include neighborhood justice centers and divorce mediation. The growth in prepaid legal care plans will require increased numbers of specialists to deal with new problems involving such areas as Social Security and worker's compensation.

## Geographic Job Index

Work as a lawyer can be found in virtually every city or town in the United States. The most prestigious private firms and largest corporations are naturally located in or near large cities. Work for the federal government is concentrated in Washington, DC, although many U.S. agencies maintain offices in other large population centers. There is a United States Attorney in every state of the union, as well as in Puerto Rico, Guam and the Virgin Islands. State government employment is most often found in the state capital or in the state's largest cities.

## Major Employers

**CORPORATIONS** hire in-house counsel to handle contracts, stock offerings, real estate transactions, labor relations, compliance with government regulations, and any other corporate business for which a lawyer's training is necessary.

**GOVERNMENT**, state and local—need lawyers to conduct both civil and criminal procedures on their behalf.

firms do not adhere to established timetables. Getting hired is often a matter of making the right contacts and being in the right place at the right time. The hiring criteria are different, too; many of these firms view academic performance as much less important than personality and street smarts.

## CORPORATE PRACTICE

Attorneys who work for corporations may wear almost as many hats as their counterparts in private practice. Depending on the size and major business of a corporation, the corporate attorney would be a generalist, coordinating the activities of in-house and outside specialists in many areas of law, or might spend his or her entire career practicing in a highly specialized area of the law.

Areas of specialization for corporate attorneys might include antitrust law, consumer issues, environmental/energy issues, government contracts, government relations, insurance, international law, litigation, personnel/labor relations, product liability, real estate, securities and finance, or tax.

Whether a generalist or a specialist, the corporate attorney does a lot of business planning with the employer. This is different from the practice of a private law firm, where the emphasis is on solving legal problems. The corporate attorney attempts to help the employer plan the affairs of the company so that problems do not arise and the goals of the corporation are achieved in a lawful manner.

Most large corporations do not require specific undergraduate or law school curricula from applicants to their law departments. However, in many cases a business degree or some business background is helpful. Depending on the business of the corporation or the concerns of a specific division in a large law department, a technical undergraduate degree may be required. These would typically include the various areas of engineering and science, and are especially important for an attorney involved in patent law.

## Qualifications

*Personal:* A logical mind. A high moral character. The ability to get along with and work well with others. Tolerance for the sometimes bothersome bureaucratic procedures that are inherent to corporate practice.

*Professional:* A doctorate of jurisprudence. A license in the state or states in which you will practice. Any additional degrees or training required to follow a particular specialty, such as technical undergraduate degrees for patent law. A firm grasp of the fundamental principles of the law and professional ethics. Excellent research and writing skills.

## Career Paths

Although it is impossible to generalize about career paths in corporations, many large law departments do have very structured paths which attorneys are expected to follow. This would usually begin with some sort of training program for one or more years, which gives the attorney an opportunity to become accustomed to the corporation's business procedures and to learn about the various activities of the law department. Work would be done in several areas of law under some supervision. The attorney could then expect to move into a particular area of specialty within the law department and gradually progress to higher levels of responsibility, perhaps including a supervisory position.

In smaller law departments, one might expect a less formal training or introductory period, and greater responsibility from the beginning. There would also be less opportunity to move into a higher position in a smaller corporation. Both small and large corporations sometimes offer attorneys the opportunity to move out of the law department and into other areas, such as planning, sales, or management. In such cases the opportunities often depend on the interests and initiative of the attorney.

PRIVATE LAW FIRMS employ lawyers to deal with individual and corporate clients in every conceivable area of law.

## How to Break Into the Field

### CORPORATE LAW

All large corporate law departments have organized procedures for recruiting, and most will interview at law schools. Smaller corporations sometimes interview on campus, but will more frequently advertise openings. The smaller the law department, the more likely it is that the employer will prefer attorneys with experience. However, there is a definite trend toward hiring new people directly from law schools. Students should be alert for these opportunities, particularly in businesses experiencing rapid growth. Anyone interested in working for a corporation should not wait for announcements of openings but should do research on possible employers and contact them directly by sending to the head of the law department a résumé and a cover letter that includes the reasons for your interest in the firm.

### GOVERNMENT SERVICE

Some federal government departments and agencies interview on campus, although recruiting visits have been cut back in recent years. Other departments, including the Department of Justice, require that an application be submitted. Candidates in whom there is interest are then asked to come in for an interview at regional offices throughout the country. Your law school placement office can supply more detailed information about federal hiring practices, as well as such special programs as the honors program, through which some of the most desirable entry-level positions are filled.

Many of the larger prosecutors' offices conduct interviews on law school campuses in the fall for permanent placement positions beginning the following year. For those students who do not obtain an on-campus interview or who wish to apply to an office that does not have such recruitment efforts, it is best to send a résumé and cover letter to the personnel office, the attorney in charge of hiring, or First Assistant District Attorney. Participation in a criminal law clinic is an especially valuable credential when seeking work in the area.

Some attorney general, city solicitors, and agency offices will interview on law school campuses in the fall for the following year; others may list openings with law schools as they become available. However, many state and city agencies never contact law schools but do hire attorneys at different times throughout the year. The best approach to take is to send a résumé and cover letter directly to each agency or office that interests you and then follow up with a phone call to determine whether any positions exist and the status of your application. It should be remembered that many government civil law offices, both state and local, are controlled by civil service laws. Law students and graduates interested in government careers should be careful to take the civil service exams when they are offered so that they can be ranked on the approved lists.

**PRIVATE PRACTICE**

There is only one sure formula for getting a job with a large corporate law firm: good grades at a prestigious law school. Large firms typically fill their openings through on-campus interviews, and they strongly prefer to hire students from those schools at which they recruit. If your school does not have a large on-campus recruiting program, a letter-writing campaign to large firms in your geographic area may net you some interviews, but only if you have superb grades or law review experience. Timing is critical, too; large firms do virtually all of their hiring during the August to November recruiting season. It is also important to begin this process during the fall of your second year of law school, because many firms fill most of their permanent openings by making offers to students who have worked for them as summer associates following their second year of law school.

Unlike large firms, which have predictable and recurring hiring needs, small firms usually hire new lawyers only occasionally, and then only when their needs are immediate. Consequently these

## Job Responsibilities

### Entry Level

In some very large corporate law departments, the beginning attorney's job might resemble an entry job in a large law firm. There will be little or no client contact, and a great deal of research and memo writing, possibly on a very narrow area of the law, or even on one case. However, even in large companies, most corporate jobs involve taking on a great deal of responsibility right away, including client contact as well as whatever research and writing is necessary to handle one's own caseload.

### Moving Up

If an attorney stays in the law department, he or she will begin to work on more difficult and important matters, with perhaps more emphasis on business planning. There will also be responsibility for supervising the work of junior lawyers, and for hiring outside counsel when necessary, specifying the work to be done by them and examining all billing to be sure that the corporation has gotten the services it has been asked to pay for.

# GOVERNMENT SERVICE

Practicing law for the government can be both a satisfying and a stimulating career choice. Government attorneys are important public servants dedicated to improving the public welfare and preserving the integrity of our judicial system. Government cases often raise challenging legal questions of constitutional dimensions as well as interesting procedural problems. The work requires an attorney who can think analytically, speak and write effectively, and research thoroughly.

With some 5000 lawyers, the U.S. Department of Justice has been described as the largest law office in the world. Its principal function is to represent the United States in court. (The day-to-day lawyering of the federal government—negotiating contracts, providing government officials with legal advice, etc.—is done by lawyers in the office of the general counsel of a department or agency.) There are 93 U.S. Attorneys who function regionally and perform the bulk of the department's litigation; their work is guided by a central staff in Washington, DC. Special case areas such as antitrust, tax, and civil rights are handled by separate divisions within the department. These are based in Washington, DC.

Other federal agencies that employ lawyers include the Securities and Exchange Commission, which monitors and enforces compliance with federal securities laws; the Federal Trade Commission, which is charged with ensuring fair market competition and consumer protection; and the Federal Reserve Board, which is involved with federal regulation of the nation's banking system.

For state and local governments, lawyers can work either in criminal prosecution or in civil law.

Prosecuting attorneys bear an important responsibility in helping to protect society and, at the same time, assuring that accused persons are given fair and impartial treatment within the criminal justice system. Their work is varied and demanding. It requires both an understanding of the procedures governing the trial of criminal matters as well as a knowledge of state or local statutory law and court precedents.

Criminal practice of this nature entails frequent appearances in court, either before a judge or a jury, to argue the legal questions that have arisen and finally to present evidence in the trial of the case. In addition, the work in a district attorney's office involves a range of other important decisions, including determining the validity of arrest procedures, assessing the factual merits of an investigation, and deciding whether to pursue a matter to trial or to bargain for a guilty plea.

State and municipal governments, because of their size and the number of services they provide, need attorneys in almost every specialty area of civil law. Housing, transportation, welfare, mental health, and family services are examples of government services, each of which is governed by its own body of laws.

Attorneys are essential to the provision of these services and to the resolution of a variety of other problems and questions, such as construction contracts, employee disputes, environmental issues, and financial arrangements.

## Qualifications

*Personal:*   Dedication to public service. Reliability. Integrity. For criminal prosecutors, the ability to deal with the consequences of criminal brutality. Ability to work well under pressure and with minimal supervision.

*Professional:*   Knowledge of law and procedure, especially as related to the subject area of practice. Excellent writing and communications skills.

## Career Paths

Some lawyers remain in government service throughout their careers; others get their early experience with the government and then move on to private or corporate practice; still others move back and forth between government service and other areas of practice.

Lawyers, like all employees who work for the federal government, are assigned a civil service grade. With promotions and continued service your grade (and the pay scale attached to it) rises. In general, promotions within the federal government will net you a wider area of responsibility, more difficult and interesting cases, and supervisory or administrative positions. Lawyers who wish to leave federal employment find that their skills and experience are applicable to private or corporate practice.

There are attorneys who chose to do prosecutorial work for most of their careers and there are others who leave the district attorneys' offices after several years. The litigation experience acquired in a prosecutor's office provides an excellent background for any other litigation or criminal justice position. Many attorneys apply the experience they have gained to the private practice of law.

Those who hold civil law jobs for state or local governments can move into agencies with wider scope, or into supervisory or administrative positions. Those who choose to leave find that their experience is well-respected by the private sector; many attorneys are able to secure positions with law firms and corporations.

## Job Responsibilities

### Entry Level

**THE BASICS:**   Legal research. Familiarizing yourself with cases and issues. Drafting briefs and memorandums.

**MORE CHALLENGING DUTIES:**   Discussing approaches to a case with other attorneys. Taking depositions. Preparing witnesses. Court appearances. Responding to inquiries from other attorneys, legal employees, or the public.

### Moving Up

The competence you display in the performance of your duties is the key to advancement. But winning cases or decisions is not the only thing that counts in the public sector. You must also understand the goals of your agency or division and must work not only toward the successful resolution of your own assignments, but toward the overall achievement of your group.

## PRIVATE PRACTICE

The private practice of law offers an exceedingly wide range of career opportunities. No other profession encompasses a greater variety of work experiences than may be found in our country's 168,000 legal establishments—a term that includes small general practice firms, large multi-office firms, and every type and size in between. Such diversity defies generalization, except in the broadest sense; however, private law practice as a whole is clearly a

# OTHER AREAS OF PRACTICE

There are three additional major areas of practice that lawyers may choose: politics, public interest law, and teaching.

Jobs in politics include lobbying and legislative positions. An experienced lawyer may choose to run for political office.

Lobbyists are responsible for presenting the positions of the client they represent—which may be a corporation, a trade or professional association, or a public interest advocacy group—to legislative and regulatory bodies, and to government executive departments at federal, state, and even local levels. Successful lobbyists are gregarious and have high energy and enthusiasm. It is a hectic job, sometimes conducted literally in the lobby of a legislative body. A lobbyist must be informed and articulate on the issues in question, and persuasive in presentation—both oral and written—of the client's point of view.

For those with a keen interest in the legislative process, positions on the staffs of legislators and legislative committees are available in Washington, DC, and in the 50 state capitals, as well as with elected officials in the nation's largest cities. The work includes researching and drafting legislation, and dealing with outside lobbyists who may be trying to influence your legislator. If you work for an individual legislator, you may also handle legislative aspects of constituent questions and draft the technical portions of newsletters for the home or state district, as well as advise the legislator on legal issues. Work on a committee is similar, but limited, of course, to the specialized area of the committee's work.

Public interest lawyers represent indigent persons in civil matters, defend indigent persons accused of a crime, or work for one of the many public interest groups that seek to advance their special interests through the legal process.

The Legal Aid Society and the Legal Services Corporation provide lawyers for persons unable to afford counsel to represent them in family and divorce matters, child support claims, probate and other civil matters. Similarly, public defenders—who may be hired by the local government or for whose services local government may contract through a private agency such as the Legal Aid Society—fulfill the obligation of government to provide an attorney for every person charged with a criminal offense, regardless of ability to pay. Lawyers who choose either of these areas of practice must have a willingness to be overworked and underpaid; there are always more cases than lawyers. And the lawyer's need to see justice done must be strong enough to overcome the sheer quantity of human trouble and misery with which he or she must come into contact.

Those who work for public interest groups such as the NAACP, the Sierra Club Legal Defense Fund, and others, spend their time advancing the interests of their group through lobbying, arguing high-impact test litigation, or advising advocates of their group on the legal aspects of their group's aims. Positions with these groups are at a premium, but showing an interest early through volunteer work can help the beginning lawyers find positions that will enable them to work for causes in which they believe.

Teaching is an area that lawyers come to after they have had some experience in private or corporate practice, or with government. As a rule, no special degrees are required beyond the J.D. (Juris Doctor) that is conferred on all law school graduates, although teachers frequently hold an LL.M. (Master of Legal Letters) degree in a specialty area, such as tax or antitrust law. A commitment to the philosophy of the law, to legal education, and to academic research is necessary to make a successful career in teaching. Many teachers, even those with full-time positions, continue to do some outside legal work, either performing services for government or establishing a relationship with a private law firm.

## ADDITIONAL INFORMATION

### Salaries

Large private practices offer the highest starting salaries for beginning associates—an average of $36,000 per year. Corporations

booming business, with gross revenues increasing at a rate of more than 12 percent annually.

Significant among the reasons for this rapid growth rate are the removal of restrictions on attorney advertising; increased numbers of legal clinics and prepaid legal services plans that provide legal services to middle-income groups; and the growing complexity of the economy. These factors have also promoted increased public awareness of individual and collective rights, which in turn provides more work for more attorneys.

Most large law firms are divided into departments along practice lines such as corporate, litigation, real estate, tax, trusts and estates. New associates are usually assigned to one department immediately, but may be given the opportunity in some firms to try out work from a variety of departments before their marriage to a particular area of practice.

Small firms are the backbone of our country's legal system. They provide legal services to small businesses, as well as specialized services for many larger companies. In addition, they handle legal problems for individual clients, including real estate transactions, divorces and other domestic relations issues, estate planning and drafting of wills, personal injury actions, ad defense against criminal charges.

## Qualifications

*Personal:*   Objectivity. A high regard for precision and detail. Good organizational abilities. Empathy. Ability to think on your feet and speak well. Physical and mental stamina. Ability to be a team player.

*Professional:*   Excellent legal research and writing skills. Finely honed analytical skills. Counseling and negotiating skills.

## Career Paths

In private practice you are either an associate or a partner. An associate is an employee; a partner is a part-owner of the firm. Because of increasing specialization, a few attorneys with in-depth knowledge in a narrow field may be designated permanent associates, but this is only an option in a few very large firms. In large firms, if you are not designated a partner in five to ten years, you are expected to find other employment. At small firms the arrangements are much less hierarchical, and the competition for partnerships is less acute. After several years in private practice attorneys may opt for a corporate spot or for government service, or political or public interest work.

## Job Responsibilities

### Entry Level

**THE BASICS:**   Legal research and writing. Large firms: rotation through departments, or work on narrow aspects of large cases. Small firms: some client contact from the beginning.

**MORE CHALLENGING DUTIES:**   Large firms: some client contact; responsibility for small cases and projects in their entirety or for more complex aspects of large cases; less structured assignments. Small firms—involvement in all phases of the litigation process.

### Moving Up

There is no magic pathway to partnership in a large firm. However, hard work, the ability to get along well with clients and to bring in new ones, and the firm's needs in the associate's area of expertise are all key components. Upward mobility does not cease once an associate becomes a partner, although there are no subsequent title designations to denote prominence. In general, those partners who are responsible for the firm's biggest clients and the most lucrative areas of practice have the strongest voice in firm management and receive the largest shares of the firm's profits.

Opportunities for upward mobility in small firms vary considerably, so it is important for the beginning associate to assess the firm structurally to determine the long-range prospects. Nearly all small firms place great emphasis on a person's ability to bring in new business; in many, a substantial client base is a prerequisite to partnership.

offer the next highest wages, with an average starting wage of $33,000 per year. In government service a beginning lawyer can expect to earn from $20,000 to $25,000 annually. In public interest work and some legislative positions, salaries can be quite low, in the $12,000 to $15,000 per year range.

## Working Conditions

*Hours:*   All lawyers work long hours—45 to 50 hours per week is common. Lawyers with large private practice firms, however, often put in much longer hours. In all legal work there will be peak periods—when an important case is being readied for trial, or when a business is negotiating an important contract or merger.

*Environment:*   A lawyer's office can be anything from a hand-somely appointed private office in an exclusive building to a battered desk and a chair in a legal clinic in a poor neighborhood. Most lawyers, however, will have surroundings that fall somewhere between these two extremes.

*Workstyle:*   Your workstyle will depend largely on your job. Some lawyers spend most of their time in research and writing, others (such as public defenders) in court, others conferring with clients and other lawyers.

*Travel:*   Travel can vary considerably, but in general it is reserved for more experienced lawyers. A corporate lawyer may be sent to other branches of the company to investigate a series of contracts; lawyers for the federal government may travel to another part of the country to interview witnesses in a case, but a great deal of travel for a beginning lawyer is unusual.

## Internships

You will find internships available for nearly every area of law. Many are paying jobs, others offer school credit, still others are volunteer positions. The best place to find out about opportunities is through your law school placement office. If no formal internships exist in the area of your interest, the placement officers may be able to point you in the right direction. Any work experience you are able to garner will help you in your search for full-time employment after graduation. Internships with government agencies and public interest groups tend to be on a volunteer basis. If you must earn money during the summer in order to continue your education, the financial aid office may be able to assist you with finding alternative funding so that you can still get some valuable work experience.

The most formal internship programs exist with large private practice firms. Indeed, students who aspire to large firm practice may find offers of permanent employment difficult to obtain if they have not clerked for a large firm the previous summer. Large firms often go to great lengths to win the favor of top-ranking students.

## Judicial Clerkships

Judicial clerkships represent a unique opportunity for new law school graduates to spend an additional year or two learning the law and the judicial process from an expert or scholar—the judge. A clerkship is a mutually beneficial arrangement. The clerk has the opportunity to work one-to-one with and to learn from this scholar, and at the same time to refine basic legal skills. The judge has an eager, bright, articulate new graduate who not only handles the time-consuming jobs of researching points of law and writing the findings into memorandums, but who is able to discuss the issues, act as a sounding board, and play devil's advocate. At its best, a clerkship provides the opportunity to work directly with, study with, and reason with the judge, and to learn the thinking and rationale behind some very difficult decisions. It is an opportunity for a new attorney to get the best possible postgraduate training. Many believe that there is no greater learning experience and no better way to begin a legal career.

Federal clerkships, especially those with higher courts, are the most prestigious, but any clerkship is of immeasurable value. The work sharpens analytic skills and strenghtens writing skills by requiring you to stretch yourself to meet the demands of a sharp and experienced mentor. And it can be an incredible boost to your career. Those who have clerked will be offered plum positions, and the experience puts you into a close working relationship with people who can be important contacts throughout your career.

The competition for clerkships is intense—requiring submission not only of a résumé and school transcript, but of samples of legal writing as well. The final hurdle is the personal interview with the judge, and here chemistry and style will come into play. However, persistence and determination in finding a clerkship can pay off in a greatly enhanced legal career.

## Recommended Reading

**BOOKS**

*After Law School? Finding a Job in a Tight Market* by Saul Miller, Little Brown & Company: 1978

*The American Lawyer Guide to Leading Law Firms*, compiled by *The American Lawyer* staff: 1983

*From Law Student to Lawyer: A Career Planning Manual* by Frances Utley with Gary A. Munneke, American Bar Association: 1984

*Good Works: A Guide to Social Change Careers*, Karen Aptakin, ed., Center for Study of Responsive Law: 1980

*How to Start and Build a Law Practice*, 2nd edition. by Jay G. Foonberg, American Bar Association: 1984

*I'd Rather Do It Myself—How to Set Up Your Own Law Firm* by Stephen Gillers, Law Journal Press: 1980

*Lawyering: A Realistic Approach to Legal Practice* by James C. Freund, Doubleday & Company: 1982

*The Lawyer in Modern Society*, 2nd edition. by Vern Countryman, Ten Finman, and Theodore J. Schneyer, Little Brown & Company: 1976

*The Lawyers* by Martin Mayer, Greenwood Press: 1980

*Lions of the Eighties: The Inside Story of the Powerhouse Law Firms* by Paul Hoffman, Doubleday & Company: 1982

*The Making of a Public Profession* by Frances Kahn Zemans and Victor G. Rosenblum, American Bar Foundation: 1981

*Martindale-Hubbell Law Directory*, Martindale-Hubbell, Inc.: revised annually

*Miller's Court* by Arthur Miller, Houghton Mifflin Company: 1982

*Opportunities in Law Careers* by Gary A. Munneke, VGM Career Horizons: 1981

*The Partners* by James B. Stewart, Simon and Schuster: 1983

*Stating Your Case: How to Interview for a Job as a Lawyer* by Joseph Ryan, West Publishing Company: 1982

*The Washington Want Ads: A Guide to Legal Careers in the Federal Government*, Moira K. Griffin, ed., American Bar Association: revised annually

*Women in Law* by Cynthia Fuchs, Anchor Press/Doubleday: 1983

**PERIODICALS**

*The American Lawyer* (monthly), AM-LAW Publishing Corporation, 205 Lexington Avenue, New York, NY 10016.

*The National Law Journal* (weekly), 111 Eighth Avenue, New York, NY 10011.

*Student Lawyer* (monthly), American Bar Association, 750 North Lake Shore Drive, Chicago, IL 60611.

### Professional Associations

The American Bar Association
1155 East 60th Street
Chicago, IL 60637

National Association of Attorneys General
444 North Capitol Street, N.W.
Suite 403
Washington, DC 20001

National District Attorneys Association
708 Pendleton Street
Alexandria, VA 22134

National Legal Aid and Defenders Association
2100 M Street, N.W.
Suite 1601
Washington, DC 20037

# INTERVIEW

**Eugune J. Majeski, Age 66**
**Founding Partner**
**Ropers, Majeski, Kohn, Bentley, Wagner and Kane, Red-
wood City, CA**

I started the "adventure" as the youngest lawyer in a San Francisco admiralty firm. At that time I knew absolutely nothing about admiralty law—because I had gone to school in Chicago, where there was no great emphasis on admiralty law. But the interesting thing about law is that you don't have to know the specialty in order to become a reasonably good lawyer, because you learn on the job; it's one of the last existing apprenticeship professions.

From the admiralty firm I went to another firm where I began to learn something about litigation, which is, I think, more art than law. I stayed with that firm for three years, generally working for one of the older partners. It was he who decided—30 years ago—to start our firm, and he apparently needed someone to carry his briefcase. I started in that capacity, but when there were only two of us, it was very easy for me quickly to become a "name" partner. We thought we would have a kind of small-town friendly litigation practice, but we are now a large-city litigating firm, because the large city grew around us.

Our firm is involved in all kinds of litigation, except for criminal work. I have principally tried cases in the fields of product liability, malpractice defense, and other civil areas, including actions for libel and slander. About nine out of ten civil cases are now disposed of without trial, though. You see, we have now reached the point where the underlying assumption of many judges is that litigants don't really have to use the court at all because they really should settle everything.

I think that potential lawyers should examine themselves carefully, to be sure that they really want to be a lawyer rather than that they just like the idea of being a lawyer, because the reality is quite different. You put in a lot of hours and you work hard, and you should not be misled into thinking that it's always a joyful, wonderful, exhilarating experience. It is all this, in part, but because the trial is just the tip of the iceberg, and for every day in court you probably spend ten days in preparation, you can see that a lot of the work is drudgery. And it's an even worse situation now, since most cases are now settled out of court.

The satisfaction in litigation is not so much in winning as in doing well in light of your own standards. You may have lost the case, but if you know that you lost it for a lot less than anyone else would have lost it you can be satisfied. Often you know that because of your intervention a more just result occurred. We all recall our great wins, but many other things also give us a feeling of satisfaction.

# NEWSPAPER PUBLISHING

D ESPITE the fact that we're living in an age in which satellites, cables, and computer systems are important tools of communications networks, the most detailed and, some say, relied-upon source of news is still the newspaper. Becoming a star reporter on a major metropolitan daily is the career dream of many journalism majors, but the hard, cold truth is that only the most talented find their way onto the staffs of papers like *The New York Times, The Washington Post,* or *The Wall Street Journal.* Fewer still are the Woodwards and Bernsteins who achieve hero status. Nonetheless, there are plenty of opportunities to distinguish yourself in this profession. Besides reporting, there are other job areas at newspapers. They include:

- **Editing**
- **Advertising Space Sales**
- **Circulation**

Although taking a solid core of writing, editing, and mass communications courses is invaluable, you will score extra points at a job interview if you can point to a subject in which you are especially well-versed. Business, political science and government, economics, and technology are all areas of expertise that are in demand.

Newspapers may still be printed on newsprint with ink, but technological advances are very much in evidence in the industry. In the offices of all large papers, and many small ones, video display terminals (VDTs) have replaced typewriters and overflowing wastebaskets. Production and printing processes have been streamlined and accelerated.

## Job Outlook

*Job Openings Will Grow:*   As fast as average

*Competition For Jobs:*   Keen

*New Job Opportunities:*   Videotex, a subscription cable service that began operating in 1983, offers news lovers the chance to read up-to-the-minute stories on their TV screens without waiting for the next edition of the paper. Recent graduates with communications backgrounds are being hired by newspapers who own videotex services to summarize and distill print stories into shorter video formats.

## Geographic Job Index

The largest, most influential newspapers are the metropolitan dailies, which are published in major cities. Smaller cities often have dailies, although these may have much simpler formats than metropolitan papers. Plenty of suburban and local papers, usually weeklies, are published nationwide, and these are most receptive to rookie reporters and first-time job-hunters.

## Who the Employers Are

There are 1711 daily newspapers and over 7000 weeklies in the United States. Only 35 papers have circulations over 250,000; the majority fewer than 50,000 readers.

LARGE CIRCULATION NEWSPAPERS have the biggest staffs, the widest readership, and the highest ad sales revenues; consequently, they are also the most difficult places to get a job, especially for the inexperienced. Some are independently owned; others are one of several newspapers owned by a chain.

Although most papers owned by a newspaper group make their own hiring decisions, some movement of employees does occur among the various papers within a group; when a new paper is purchased, the parent company often moves in its own talent, especially at senior levels.

LOCAL NEWSPAPERS serve the needs of smaller cities, most suburban communities, and many rural areas. Besides news coverage, many have the same departments found in bigger papers, such as entertainment, sports, cooking, and life-style. Recently, many have been purchased by newspaper chains.

A growing number of local papers are financed entirely by advertising and distributed free. They are often published in resort communities during the tourist season and feature articles on local history, current events, and sports. Although jobs on these "throwaways" tend to be very low-paying, these papers have high standards and offer good opportunities to gain experience.

WIRE SERVICES supply syndicated stories and features to subscribing newspapers. Many papers, including the largest, use these services as a means of expanding their news coverage. Wire services employ reporters and writers.

TRADE NEWSPAPERS address the needs and interests of professionals in a particular field or industry. Some, such as *W*,

*Variety,* and *Advertising Age,* are sold on newstands, but most are available only to subscribers. These publications provide excellent opportunities to develop writing and reporting skills and to get the experience necessary to move on to a daily newspaper.

## Major Employers

### LARGE CIRCULATION NEWSPAPERS
*The Chicago Sun-Times* (Murdoch—New American Publishing Company)
*The Chicago Tribune* (The Tribune Company)
*The Detroit Free Press* (Knight-Ridder Newspapers)
*The Detroit News* (Evening News Association)
*The Los Angeles Times* (The Times-Mirror Company)
*The New York Daily News* (The Tribune Company)
*The New York Post* (Murdoch—New American Publishing Company)
*The New York Times* (The New York Times Company)
*The Philadelphia Inquirer* (Knight-Ridder Newspapers)
*USA Today* (Gannett Newspapers)
*The Wall Street Journal* (Dow Jones Company)
*The Washington Post* (The Washington Post Company)

### NEWSPAPER PUBLISHING GROUPS
Gannett Newspapers (87 papers)
Donrey Media Group (48 papers)
Knight-Ridder Newspapers (31 papers)
Freedom Newspapers (29 papers)
Newhouse Newspapers (14 papers)
Hearst Newspapers (8 papers)
The Times-Mirror Company (6 papers)
Murdoch—New American Publishing Company (5 papers)

## How to Break into the Field

Some recent graduates land jobs at urban dailies, but these applicants often have exceptional credentials and good contacts who can make introductions for them. If you have neither of these, you must be willing to start at a small paper and work your way up.

Your best foot-in-the-newspaper-door is a summer job or internship. Barring this, you should write the editor or department head of papers that interest you and follow up with a phone call. Phone contact is essential to landing an interview, because editors are often too busy to respond to letters.

Carefully read the papers you intend to contact and familiarize yourself with their format, departments, and style. If you are interested in a reporting position, prepare a portfolio with samples of your best work. For jobs in advertising, sales experience of any kind is a plus.

A master's degree in journalism does not guarantee you the job of your choice. Some employers value the credential; others are more interested in your experience. A graduate degree from a highly regarded school can be an introduction to alumni who either are in hiring positions or can recommend you to colleagues who are. A graduate program in journalism can be especially valuable for graduates of liberal arts schools that do not offer a journalism curriculum.

# REPORTING

Investigative work may be the most fascinating and dramatic type of reporting, but it isn't the bread and butter of journalism. Stories about traffic accidents, local politics, school board meetings, strikes, zoning disputes, the opening of new businesses are more typical of daily fare. However, these stories require the same researching, interviewing, analyzing, and writing skills—under the pressure of a deadline, of course—that you will use when you make your first big scoop.

The duties of a beginning reporter vary according to the size of the paper. At a large paper, you would begin as a news assistant, checking information for more experienced reporters while being trained on the job. At a small paper, you'll be given simple reporting assignments immediately.

As your skills improve, you may be given a beat to cover—perhaps the courts, the local police precinct, the school system, or an area in which you've developed some expertise. You will be responsible for story ideas, which means establishing a good network of contacts who will call you when an event occurs, a crisis is brewing, or a human interest story comes along.

## Qualifications

*Personal:* Curiosity. High energy level. Ability to produce under pressure. Willingness to take risks. Ability to withstand criticism. Dedication. Courage.

*Professional:* Typing. Ability to use (or to learn to use) a VDT. Photography skills helpful. Ability to obtain accurate information. Ability to explain complex issues in concise, logical language. Excellent grammar and writing skills.

## Career Paths

| LEVEL | JOB TITLE | EXPERIENCE NEEDED |
|-------|-----------|-------------------|
| Entry | News assistant, major metropolitan newspaper | College degree |
|  | Reporter, small newspaper |  |
| 2 | Reporter, medium-size newspaper | 2-3 years |
| 3 | Reporter, major metropolitan newspaper | 3-5 years |
|  | Editor, small newspaper | 3-5 years |
|  | Editor, medium-size newspaper | 5-7 years |
|  | Editor, major metropolitan newspaper | 10+ years |

## Job Responsibilities

### Entry Level

**THE BASICS:** News assistants at large-circulation newspapers: Filing. Clipping articles. Moving copy. Answering phones. Reporters at small newspapers: Rewriting press releases. Writing simple items such as obituaries.

**MORE CHALLENGING DUTIES:** News assistants at large-circulation newspapers: Doing research. Reporting and writing for special editions or supplements. Reporters at small newspapers: Covering community meetings and events. Reporting and writing stories under your own by-line. Taking photographs to accompany your stories.

### Moving Up

Your progress will depend on your skills and the size of the newspaper. A solid record of accurate, well-written articles will build your reputation, but a prize-winning story or one whose significance reaches beyond your local area can bring your work to the attention of an editor at a larger, more prestigious paper. Routine assignments don't often lead to such opportunities, so it is up to you to discover them.

Many young reporters leapfrog from one paper to another every few years to increase the depth and variety of their experience. Others develop an area of expertise by staying in a particular department. It's only after you've proved yourself to be highly competent, accurate, and reliable in your work that you'll be considered by major metropolitan dailies.

## EDITING

Even though an editor has prestige and power and commands a higher salary, many reporters are reluctant to trade in their by-line for a desk job. Still, if you prove yourself to be a talented word-smith with impeccable judgment, you will be viewed by management as a prime candidate for the editing staff.

Editors work with staff writers, reporters, and photographers; they assign stories, review copy, and give advice to reporters on legal and ethical questions. They're responsible for what the newspaper prints, and must scrutinize and question the content of their reporters' work.

The following editorial positions are found at major papers; smaller publications have a more simplified editorial hierarchy, with responsibilities for specialized areas combined or eliminated entirely.

NEWS EDITORS decide whether a story will be covered and the degree of prominence it will receive. The largest papers have separate desks for city, state, national, and foreign news.

DEPARTMENT EDITORS oversee a particular section, such as sports, life-style, entertainment, or business, and often write regular columns in their area of specialization.

EDITORIAL PAGE EDITORS meet regularly to determine the position the paper will take on important national, regional, and local issues, as well as which opinion pieces and essays will be featured on their pages. A newspaper's editorial policy often influences politicians and corporate leaders as well as its readers.

SUNDAY EDITORS coordinate the various special sections that appear on Sunday and provide any additional coverage needed for the largest edition of the week.

COPY EDITORS are expert in grammar, spelling, punctuation, and word usage. They can turn bland, choppy, or illogical copy into a readable piece. Copy editors also write heads (headlines)—a special talent. Unlike other editing positions, copy editing does not necessarily require prior reporting experience, nor does it usually lead to senior editing positions.

# ADVERTISING SPACE SALES

Because most newspapers rely on advertising revenue rather than subscriptions or single copy sales for financial viability, a hardworking, creative sales department is a must. A successful salesperson first has to convince a potential client that the newspaper will provide his or her product with the widest possible exposure to the right audience.

Newspaper advertisements fall into two categories: display and classified. Display ads, found throughout the newspaper, are often illustrated and can cover an entire page or spread. The classified section advertises help wanted, merchandise for sale, real estate, etc. It's often easier to land an entry-level position in classified ad sales than in display sales, especially on a major metropolitan daily.

As competition for advertising dollars has become keener, the space sales department has had to become more organized and "scientific" in the way it conducts business. Because more and more newspapers are requiring applicants to have a college degree and sales know-how to land a job in space sales, it is rapidly becoming an attractive opportunity for highly motivated, personable, and energetic graduates.

## Qualifications

*Personal:*   An outgoing personality. Resourcefulness. Initiative. Persistence.

*Professional:*   Good phone manner. Typing. Written and oral communications skills. Understanding of advertising techniques. Familiarity with or sales experience in an industry that advertises in print, particularly the retail business.

## Career Paths

| LEVEL | JOB TITLE | EXPERIENCE NEEDED |
|---|---|---|
| Entry | Account executive (display) or Telemarketing sales representative (classified), small or medium-size newspaper | College degree |
| | Account executive (display) or telemarketing sales experience representative (classified), major metropolitan newspaper | 1-2 years' sales |
| 2 | Advertising manager, small or medium-size newspaper | 4-6 years |
| | Advertising manager, major metropolitan newspaper | 7-10 years |
| 3 | Advertising director (display or classified), small or medium-size newspaper | 10 years |
| | Advertising director (display or classified), major metropolitan newspaper | 15+ years |

## Job Responsibilities

### Entry Level

**THE BASICS:**   In classified ad sales: Taking orders over the phone or from walk-in customers. In display: Assisting experienced sales personnel. Helping with correspondence, phone calls, and other detail work.

**MORE CHALLENGING DUTIES:** Soliciting the business of small clients with phone calls and visits. Making sure that ads appear in the right space at the right time.

## Moving Up

Your progress will be measured in easily definable terms: how many advertising dollars you bring in. The more small accounts you handle successfully, the more freedom you'll have in developing new business and the more major accounts you'll be given. Unlike other types of jobs, the nature of your responsibilities won't change dramatically, but as you move up you'll be dealing with more prestigious accounts and will find higher-ranking people as your client contacts. You may, however, begin specializing in a certain category of client—retail, automotive sales, employment agencies—particularly if you work for a major metropolitan pa<sub>r</sub> ⌐r with a large sales staff. Specialization allows you to develop ⌐ broad understanding of your client's needs, to service the account better and persuade the client to increase the amount of advertising he or she buys from your paper. The most experienced account executives handle national advertisers.

# CIRCULATION

No paper could exist without the circulation department, but it is an area often overlooked by job seekers. The circulation staff gets the papers out to newsstands and other distribution points and into the hands of subscribers. Circulation is responsible for recruiting carriers, seeing that papers are delivered promptly and bills are collected, and resolving customer complaints and problems. At metropolitan papers, staff members often work in satellite offices to facilitate distribution.

This diversified department determines reader demographics, analyzes what kinds of advertising and editorial information readers respond to, and seeks to increase readership. The department may conduct its own research, or may use the services of a market research firm.

The majority of jobs are in the field with larger papers. In-house circulation staffs are small and usually composed of experienced people.

## Qualifications

*Personal:*  Being well-organized. Patience with details. Plenty of energy and endurance.

*Professional:*  Diplomacy. Ability to judge character and recruit dependable carriers. Managerial skills.

## Career Paths

| LEVEL | JOB TITLE | EXPERIENCE NEEDED |
| --- | --- | --- |
| Entry | District manager | College degree |
| 2 | Branch manager | 5-10 years |
| 3 | Circulation director | 15 years |

## Job Responsibilities

### Entry Level

THE BASICS:  Keeping track of subscription record. Mapping delivery routes.

MORE CHALLENGING DUTIES:  Handling customer service. Supervising carriers. Offering your ideas to superiors on how circulation can be improved.

## Moving Up

Your success in satisfying subscribers and finding new ones are the key factors in moving up. You must demonstrate an ability to anticipate circulation problems. Developing a solid delivery track record is equally important, which may mean making deliveries yourself if a carrier quits or gets sick. An ability to manage and work with your delivery staff will also contribute to your success. If you get to the position of branch manager, you will oversee several district managers. The circulation director coordinates market research as well as the logistics of distribution.

# ADDITIONAL INFORMATION

### Salaries

Newspaper salaries vary widely. At the smallest papers, contributing reporters may be paid by the article or by the word. The highest salaries are earned by newspaper staffs that belong to the Newspaper Guild. Approximately 160 papers are unionized, including nearly all large-circulation papers. The following weekly minimum salaries are taken from the Guild's December 1983, *Collective Bargaining Manual*, which is updated monthly. These are the lowest minimums reported; some Guild papers have significantly higher minimums. An individual may be paid more, but never less, than the permitted minimum. Pay at non-Guild papers may be lower.

| | |
|---|---|
| Reporter | $184.00 (starting); $284.83 (4 years' experience). |
| Advertising salesperson (display) | $284.83 (4 years' experience). |
| Circulation district manager | $265.80 (5 years' experience), plus compensation for travel expenses; some contracts include the use of a company car. |

## Working Conditions

*Hours:*   Large dailies keep general news reporters working round-the-clock, so graveyard shift and weekend duty are unavoidable, particularly for newcomers.

Editors work long and irregular hours because they must wait for stories to come in and stay as long as is required to perfect the copy.

Nine-to-five hours are the norm in sales, although you have to be willing to adjust your schedule to accommodate clients.

Circulation people on a morning paper can begin their day as early as 4 A.M. Overtime and weekend hours are unavoidable as problems arise.

*Environment:*   Reporters usually work in a crowded bullpen area. Noisy newsrooms with clacking typewriters are passe now that VDTs are in use.

Editors work in the same environment and often in the same room as the reporting staff, although most senior editors usually have their own offices.

The sales staff has a bullpen arrangement similar to its editorial counterpart. Only a top sales executive rates a private office.

Circulation people, whether they're within the newspaper offices or in satellite offices, have only the bare necessities—a desk and a telephone.

*Workstyle:*   Reporters spend most of the day on the phone interviewing sources, or at the scene of a story. At some point in the day, you'll be back at your desk, writing and rewriting copy.

Editors spend most of their time at their desks in front of their VDTs. They also attend weekly and, at large papers, daily meetings.

Sales staffers spend a good deal of time talking to clients and making presentations to new prospects, on the phone or face to face. In classified sales, however, you'll mostly do phone solicitations.

Circulation people spend plenty of time out of the office to check up on carriers or to deliver papers to newsstands. Customer service and contacts with the home office are largely conducted by phone.

*Travel:*  Local travel is frequent for most reporters; overnight travel is rare unless a reporter is working on a special assignment.

Editors usually do more out-of-town travel than reporters, because they attend conventions and special events connected with their department or on occasion conduct interviews with VIPs.

Display sales reps do plenty of local travel, and even overnight travel if their paper serves a large geographic area. In classified sales there is minimal opportunity for even local travel.

No overnight travel is involved in circulation.

## Extracurricular Activities/Work Experience

College newspaper, yearbook, alumni
    publications—reporting, editing, layout, advertising

Society For Collegiate Journalists, Associated Collegiate
    Press, Sigma Delta Chi, National School Yearbook,
    Newspaper Association—student member

## Internship

The Newspaper Fund, Inc., sponsors a summer internship program in editing. Approximately 40 interns are placed at participating papers nationwide and gain experience in all phases of copy editing. Applicants must take an intensive copy editing course sponsored by the Newspaper Fund before they are placed. The internship is held between a student's junior and senior years. Contact: Executive Director, The Newspaper Fund Editing Internship Program, P.O. Box 300, Princeton, NJ 08540.

Both large and small papers take interns, but usually only the larger ones will pay. Contact the managing editor of the paper that interests you.

## Recommended Reading

**BOOKS**

*All the President's Men* by Bob Woodward and Carl Bernstein, Warner Books: 1976

*Goodbye Gutenburg: The Newspaper Revolution of the 1980's* by Anthony Smith, Oxford University Press: 1980

*The Great American Newspaper: The Story of the Village Voice* by Kevin McAuliffe, Charles Scribner's Sons: 1978

*The Imperial Post: The Meyers, the Grahams and the Paper That Rules Washington* by Tom Kelly, William Morrow and Company: 1983

*The Kingdom and the Power* by Gay Talese, Dell Publishing Company: 1981

*Market Guide*, Robert U. Brown, ed., Editor and Publisher Company: 1983 (information on daily newspaper markets in the U. S. and Canada)

*Newspaper Story: One Hundred Years of the Boston Globe* by Louis M. Lyons, Harvard University Press: 1971

*Page One: The Story of the City News Bureau of Chicago* by A. A. Dornfield, Academy Chicago, Ltd.: 1983

*The Typewriter Guerrillas: Close-up of Twenty Top Investigative Reporters* by John C. Behrens, Nelson Hall: 1977

*The World's Great Dailies: Profiles of Fifty Newspapers* by John C. Merrill and Hall Fisher, Hastings House Publishers: 1980

**PERIODICALS**

*Columbia Journalism Review* (bimonthly), Columbia University School of Journalism, 116th Street and Broadway, New York, NY 10027

*Editor and Publisher: The Fourth Estate* (weekly), Editor and Publisher Company, 575 Lexington Avenue, New York, NY 10022

## Professional Associations

American Newspaper Publishers Association
The Newspaper Center
Box 17407
Dulles International Airport
Washington, DC 20041

National Newspaper Association
1627 K Street, N.W.
Suite 400
Washington, DC 20036

The Newspaper Fund
P.O. Box 300
Princeton, NJ 08540

# INTERVIEWS

**Andrea Pawlyna, Age 33**
**Consumer Reporter**
*The Baltimore Sun, Baltimore,* **MD**

I enjoy the variety in my job, and I like the idea of writing stories that are useful and timely in some way. I think the most important qualities a reporter should have are a sense of outrage at injustice, an understanding of fair play, and integrity. To me, journalism is more than just a job. Even with all of its imperfections, it's still the glue that keeps any democracy intact.

I have been a reporter for about ten years. After I graduated from Columbia University's Graduate School of Journalism, I got a job as editor of a small weekly paper in upstate New York called the *Millbrook Pond Table.* I did everything, from writing the stories to taking the pictures to laying out the paper to delivering it to the printing office and then delivering it to the readers. After a year or so, I was hired by *The Poughkeepsie Journal,* a daily paper about ten miles down the road. I worked there as a reporter for almost two years, working on beats that included general assignment, politics, and the courts.

After I left the *Journal,* I came to *The Baltimore Sun* as a consumer reporter. Many of the stories I do here deal with everyday, meat-and-potatoes issues. But I'm not limited on subject matter. I write about everything from investment schemes to health spas to regulations from the Food and Drug Administration—as long as it's of interest to consumers.

One of my favorite stories involved pyramid games in Maryland. They work something like this: A promoter tries to convince people to invest a thousand dollars each in a fund with the promise that they can collect thousands more if they get two more people to each invest a thousand dollars. If you think about the mathematics involved, it doesn't take long before these pyramids lure in tremendous numbers of people. However, the only people who really end up benefiting are those on the top levels of the pyramid. Everyone else winds up losing money.

After I wrote my story, the game quickly collapsed in the state. The police arrested the ringleaders, and they were convicted, by the way. I remember feeling pretty satisfied about that one.

## Jeff Little, Age 24
## Retail Advertising Representative
### *Independent Journal*, San Rafael, CA

I went to a small liberal arts college, where I majored in business administration. My first job was selling office supplies for the Boise Cascade Corporation. My clients were retailers and dealers, and my job included supplying them with promotional materials to help sell our products directly. My interest in advertising and the satisfaction I get from working with small retailers led to my present job. I knew newspaper advertising sales would be a good way to use my background and to help retailers improve their business.

I grew up reading the *Independent Journal*, and it's fun working with a paper I know so well. It's a medium-size daily that reaches all of Marin County. This area is also served by a metropolitan daily, the *San Francisco Chronicle*, and several small, local papers.

I'm always in the office for an hour or two each morning doing paperwork, but the major part of my day is spent in the field. In this business it's important to see people. I meet with some regular advertisers every week, others every two or three weeks depending on how heavily they advertise. I also make "cold" calls, trying to get potential advertisers interested in the paper. Advertising is heaviest during the weeks before Chistmas, so in November and December it's especially important to get out to the retailers and get their business.

I deal with different kinds of accounts—a supermarket, a chain of hardware stores, shopping center merchants. Much of my time is spent keeping track of the changing needs of these accounts.

Some accounts will provide me with a prepared ad, produced by an in-house department or an ad agency. Others have a rough idea already sketched out for an ad. I advise them on what kind of design would work best with their product. A few rely on me to put the ad together from scratch. Design and layout work is time-consuming, but we have a creative services staff to do this. I tell them what the retailer and I have discussed, and they produce a finished ad. This service helps me tremendously because it encourages businesses that haven't advertised to try it.

If the first ad is good and the retailer gets a positive response from consumers, he or she will continue to advertise. So by helping an account's business grow, you help your own. You must build trust with your accounts because they rely on you to see that their ads are correct. I really do believe you can't just reserve space on a page; you've got to sell the idea.

Right now I only work with local advertisers, but I'm looking forward to the added challenge and responsibility that comes with working with national advertisers.

---

✳

---

# POLITICS

POLITICS in America is a big business. Every four years, the major political parties spend from $10 to $30 million each on the presidential campaign. To run a respectable campaign for governor or senator in the larger states takes at least $1 million. Although at times it seems only an exercise in charisma or a game of luck, politics is a highly specific and competitive field in which there are many other professionals besides the candidates who run for and win (or fail to win) office.

Over the last 25 years, politics and the media have become intimately intertwined. For the most part, the old political machine has had to make way for the "new politics": the technique of communicating a candidate's message directly to the voter without funneling it through the party organization. In response, a whole new breed of professional politicians has emerged, skilled in planning and financing mass-oriented campaigns, getting the most political mileage out of television, direct mail, and advertising.

With the arrival of the computer, the direct link between the candidate and the voter has been cemented. The computer provides the tool to create and maintain an organization that can capitalize on the image being created through the media. It allows for the breakdown of large voter lists into small, select groups; it provides a means of sending personalized letters to hundreds, even thousands of people; it monitors registration, compiles lists and information, analyzes voting patterns, and monitors membership drives.

Graduates entering the field must be interested in the political process per se, and not necessarily in the process of government. Although history, political science, and government majors have traditionally pursued political careers, journalism or communications majors and computer programmers are as likely, these days, to find openings.

There are three areas of access into the political arena: working on staff for a state or national legislator, governor, or mayor, joining a campaign, or taking a job with a public interest group or political party. Although there are many other popularly elected officials at both the state and local levels, most inherit civil service or other government staffs, and therefore do not offer comparable opportunities for the political careerist.

To break in, an internship is highly recommended. It can often serve as the stepping-stone to a paid position in a field where many entry-level employees are hired on a volunteer basis.

Movement between the three areas at all professional levels is quite common. To get ahead, you will have to develop an area of specialization, which very often entails higher education. Expertise in legislation is a route commonly taken by those with a legal bent, and requires a law degree. Other newer areas of specialization include media control, voter and legislative behavior analysis, fund raising, computer programming, and polling. Once you become a specialist, you can work for a member of Congress (or for the President) just as readily as for a public interest group or for a campaign.

## Job Outlook

*Job Openings Will Grow:*   As fast as average

*Competition for Jobs:* Keen
Expect the most competition at the highly visible lobby groups, which operate on small budgets and with small staffs. In Washington, DC, the representative from your home district and the senators from your home state are the most likely employers, especially if you have intern experience. In an election year, there will be less competition for jobs at political parties, activist groups, or on the campaigns of underdog candidates.

*New Job Opportunities:* Although both houses of Congress are limited by statute in the number of committees they may create, the number of subcommittees is not limited, and their rate of growth has averaged two per house per year since 1946. New subcommittees invariably mean more research, more issue papers, more hearings, and more jobs.

The biggest job developer, however, has been the computer. Its ability to store, sort, and selectively print reams of information has relieved volunteer staff workers on campaigns and in public interest groups from clerical work, permitting them instead to have more contact with the voters. The computer has also opened the still only partially explored realm of analysis. Its ability to index and file survey results, pertinent issue listings, correspondence records, and information on the opposition is rapidly creating new jobs for method and data analysts.

## Geographic Job Index

Washington, DC, as the seat of the nation's government, provides the highest concentration of political opportunities. Senators and representatives, congressional committees and subcommittees, the political parties, and major public interest or advocacy groups all maintain offices there. Every state capital, however, acts as a mini-Washington, with its own legislature, governor, lieutenant governor, etc. State capitals also often house campaign offices for both state and national candidates. Public interest groups and political party organizations can be found all over the country, even in the smallest of towns.

## Who the Employers Are

**LEGISLATORS AT THE NATIONAL AND STATE LEVEL** employ many staff members. Incumbent house members (in Washington, DC) are permitted up to 18 paid employees per year. Incumbent senators have a staff allowance ranging from $500,000 to $1 million per year, depending on the size of their state. This usually means a staff of between 30 and 45 employees, with up to 3 additional legislative aides employed for committee work. Majority and minority leaders at both the state and national levels maintain the largest staffs, often with offshoot staffs in various districts of their home states.

**THE REPUBLICAN AND DEMOCRATIC NATIONAL COMMITTEES** maintain headquarters in Washington, DC, as well as district offices in all major cities in the country and representatives in every county. The small permanent staffs in Washington, DC (approximately 50 at each headquarters) blossom during campaigns.

**PUBLIC INTEREST ADVOCACY GROUPS (PARTISAN AND NON-PARTISAN)** are another major employer. Among the most well-known are Common Cause, Ralph Nader's Citizen Lobby, the AFL-CIO Committee on Political Education (COPE), Business and Industry's Political Action Committee (BIPAC), the National Wildlife Federation, and the National Organization of Women (NOW).

**CAMPAIGNS** must employ large numbers of people. There are 435 members of the House of Representatives, 100 senators, 50 state governors, about 50 state senators in each state senate (Minnesota with 67 has the largest number), and approximately 300 state representatives per state (Hawaii with 400 has the most). There are

3047 county governments, which typically include an election commissioner, an attorney general, a tax assessor, and a county clerk. Although the magnitude and complexity of the election campaigns will vary widely with the size of the constituency, each of these is a popularly elected official who has run and won a campaign and probably hired people to help him or her do it.

## How to Break into the Field

Although it might take time to become involved as a paid participant in the field, politics is one of the most accessible of all careers if you are willing to volunteer your services for a short time. Internships are particularly valuable (although not an absolute necessity) in gaining entry. As an intern you make important contacts, and you can plug into the grapevine through which you will hear about job openings. As effective is having been an active member of a public interest group or national political association. Jobs are rarely advertised except by word of mouth. College graduates who have been politically active or who have been interns hold an unqualified edge over others looking to enter the political process.

If you are without the benefit of an internship, you should write a concise and carefully thought-out letter to the legislator or political party or interest group you would like to become affiliated with and request advice and the names of anyone who might have an entry-level position to fill. Follow up with a telephone call and afterward with a thank-you note.

Use your contacts. Having good contacts is one of the keys to a successful political career, and breaking into the arena is a good time to start learning the technique. Be persistent. Press for interviews. If you do not live where the jobs are, make the effort to get there so you can meet prospective employers and members of their staffs.

## International Job Opportunities

With the possible exception of foreign campaigns, international job possibilities are extremely limited. Candidates for office in

## Job Responsibilities

## Entry Level

**THE BASICS:**   Answering telephones, distributing literature, filing, typing, stuffing envelopes, hanging posters, selling tickets, bag-carrying, chauffeuring, or dog-walking.

**MORE CHALLENGING DUTIES:**   Doing basic research, attending press briefings, computer monitoring, canvassing, phone campaigning. Computer filing and indexing.

## Moving Up

Doing a superior job on routine assignments will soon pay off with recruitment into the professional group from the volunteer group. It will mean more interesting work and a greater share of political activity. Volunteer for any odd jobs that come your way. Better still, make suggestions. If you wish to go into fund raising, think of ways to raise money, and volunteer to run the projects you have in mind. Pulling off a small fund-raising project will show that you can organize well and stay within a budget. Fund raisers are to political campaigns what salespeople are to business. The goal is to make more money than their colleagues. The more contributions you can induce your candidate's supporters to make, the more you will be involved in developing major fund-raising drives, deciding not only how money is raised but also how it is spent, and determining what interest groups to cater to.

Fund raising and media coverage often go hand in hand. Establishing a rapport with the press is another avenue to promotion. Press coverage is expensive. But getting it free on the news is always risky. You must learn to balance controlled (i.e., paid-for) coverage with uncontrolled (i.e., news) coverage. A media director must have a good understanding of the opponents' campaigns as well as an astute sense of how the voting audience thinks and how much of a particular kind of coverage the candidate's campaign can use.

If your skills and interest lie in writing and research, you must be able to turn out copy that is accurate, timely, succinct, and in keeping with your candidate's point of view. Depending on the campaign, research will cover local, national, or foreign affairs issues. The more your copy is used in speeches and briefings, the more your ideas will be incorporated into the candidate's policies and image.

Campaign work requires a great deal of flexibility. If the candidate you are working for drops out of the race or loses, you must be ready to step into another candidate's campaign. Job security is not the strong point of campaigning, although the contacts you make will often be good leads for finding work elsewhere.

## LEGISLATIVE STAFF

The staff of an incumbent politician, whether at the city, state, or federal level, has two primary functions: keeping the politician (your boss) informed of his or her constituents' views, and developing legislation or policy to reflect those views. Every week, executive office holders and congressional and county legislators receive hundreds of letters from their constituents: some air complaints, some voice support, most offer opinions and suggestions. It is the staff's job to answer every one of these letters to ensure that the voter doesn't feel neglected or passed over, as well as to chart majority and minority views, changing opinions, and new trends.

Maintaining a list of supporters and voters is critical to the political life span of every elected official. Newsletters, questionnaires, and campaign materials are sent to various groups drawn from the list, especially to those who have initiated communication by phone or mail with the politician's office.

Partly through the dialogue of incoming and outgoing mail, and partly through testing the waters on frequent trips home, the attitudes of congressional members parallel those of their con-

other countries occasionally look to experienced American campaign planners to act as consultants in running their campaigns. Foreign governments will also sometimes hire political consultants to conduct electoral referendums or design media campaigns. The use of American consultants in foreign campaigning is on the rise, but only very slowly.

## CAMPAIGNING

Working on the campaign of a candidate for local, state, or national office is the most exciting way to break into the political arena. The campaign committee is responsible for all the public relations activities that establish and maintain a candidate's image. It also develops policy, raises money, and, at election time, gets out the vote.

Campaign workers, who most often start off as volunteers before moving on to paid status, are jacks-of-all-trades. The nature of the job changes to match the progress of the campaign. At the beginning, rallies, fund raisers, and picnics must be organized, the attention of the press must be caught, the personality of the candidate must be established. In the case of state-wide or national campaigns, media advance teams travel to various locations chosen for benefits or other voter-participation projects weeks before the events are scheduled to take place. Advance teams reserve the right size halls, negotiate prices, arrange accommodations and transportation, schedule media coverage, and "debug" the program of events.

Back at headquarters, direct mailings and phone campaigns help inform the public and encourage their participation, media briefings are conducted, speeches and position papers are written. In a presidential campaign with offices in every town, these tasks tend to become more specialized than in a local campaign with only a few people on the committee. As Election Day approaches, however, success for both depends on getting out the vote through door-to-door canvassing and monitoring voter turnout.

## Qualifications

*Personal:*   People oriented. Leadership qualities coupled with the ability to work well within a group. Commitment to a particular candidate or party. Energy.

*Professional:*   Writing skills, familiarity with word processing helpful. Good phone manner. Strong sense of organization, especially under pressure. Eye for the practical.

## Career Paths

| LEVEL | JOB TITLE | EXPERIENCE NEEDED |
|---|---|---|
| Entry | Volunteer, fieldworker, staff aide | College degree |
| 2 | Assistant director of volunteers, media advance team member, area fund raiser, special interest group liaison | 1-4 years (or campaigns) |
| 3 | Director of volunteers, speech writer, press secretary, media director, appointments director, district fund raiser | 3-7 years |
| 4 | Finance chairperson, counsel, campaign manager | 7-10+ years, (law degree for counsel) |

stituencies about 75 percent of the time (the number is lower for incumbents in executive offices, such as mayors or governors). The crunch comes when a senator, representative, or other elected official casts a major vote out of keeping with the views of the constituency. In that event, a good explanation must be immediately forthcoming, and the staff must anticipate the questions and formulate the replies.

## Qualifications

*Personal:*   Enthusiasm for the ideas and strengths of a particular elected official. People oriented. Ability to work well as part of a team. Drive.

*Professional:*   Good phone manner. Typing, filing, and other office skills, preferably some computer experience. Good grammar. Ability to write quickly and concisely.

## Career Paths

| LEVEL | JOB TITLE | EXPERIENCE NEEDED |
|---|---|---|
| Entry | Staff assistant | College degree and internship |
| 2 | Special assistant (research), Special assistant (constituency) | 1-4 years |
| 3 | Legislative aide, administrative aide | 3-7 years |
| 4 | Legislative director, senior analyst, press secretary | 7+ years |

## Job Responsibilities

## Entry Level

THE BASICS: Sorting mail, sending out form letters (computerized mail), compiling mailing lists, answering phones, acting as a go-for.

MORE CHALLENGING DUTIES: Answering some correspondence, following a select number of current economic and political issues, becoming acquainted with laws and procedures (in Washington, DC, this is referred to as "Hill" experience).

## Moving Up

After the first year or two of working with the mail and researching specific policy issues to the point where you have become the office specialist on them, you have to make a career choice: concentrating on legislation with the goal of becoming a legislative aide (LA) or taking increasing responsibility for office management with the aim of becoming an administrative aide (AA). The first means becoming well-versed in the key issues before Congress and the current administration. Your astuteness at judging which issues are most important, and your ability to understand the mechanisms by which to get them translated into policy, or if not that, at least into gaining good political leverage and publicity, is critical to your promotion. LA's meet and negotiate with lobbyists and representatives of other special interest groups, attend committee and subcommittee sessions, write position papers and testimonies, and help formulate new bills or other legislation. To become a legislative aide, further education in law is usually required.

Many legislative employees start in the office of an elected official and work up through the ranks by moving from one official to the next as jobs open up. Others, who stay with the same elected official, will go back and forth from the office to the campaign trail. The line between legislative assistant to the incumbent, and speechwriter or policy consultant to the candidate, is often a very fine one.

As an administrative aide, you are essentially chief of staff. To move into such a position, you must show a flair for organization and an understanding of budgeting, scheduling, and constituency management. It will be your responsibility to supervise the staff and interns; to represent the legislator at various hearings, committee meetings, and community functions; and to handle media relations.

Occasionally, the assistant to a prominent politician will move into a front seat on the political scene. (Joseph Califano, President Carter's Secretary of Health, Education, and Welfare, was a case in point, having been legislative aide to Cyrus Vance at the Pentagon.) Others become lobbyists, political consultants to business, or legislative analysts.

## PUBLIC INTEREST GROUP STAFF

The goal of an advocacy group, partisan or nonpartisan, is to persuade incumbent politicians to vote in favor of or against particular policies. Further, most actively campaign for candidates known to support certain ideas or positions. Usually, it is the small permanent staff that directs all the group's official activities; the mass membership can be counted on only to contribute numbers and money. This is as true of political parties as it is of nonpartisan and single-issue interest groups. All are clientele-conscious—by definition open, informal, and personalized. Lobbyists must combine political savvy with salesmanship. Staffs must carry out extensive research on current issues, assess strategy pro and con, and balance issue importance with the priorities of the administration and the legislature.

Monitoring voting patterns is one of the key activities of a special interest group. Another is membership drives. Most lobbies and political parties also publish nonprofit newsletters that keep their membership informed and involved. Staff members often develop an area of expertise: legislation, polling, field work, recruiting. In the smaller lobbies and parties, these activities are shared by one or two people. In larger ones, whole departments work on each area. In both cases the purpose is the same: to devise effective political action programs in order to bring about accommodation between the law and the citizenry.

## Qualifications

*Personal:* Political awareness. Self-motivation. Curiosity. Diplomacy. Outgoing, sociable personality.

*Professional:* Ability to translate data into conclusive arguments. Writing skills. Speaking skills.

## Career Paths

| LEVEL | JOB TITLE | EXPERIENCE NEEDED |
|---|---|---|
| Entry | Research assistant, press assistant, assistant field representative | College degree (internship) |
| 2 | Legislative assistant, administrative assistant, assistant for special projects, field representative | 1-4 years |
| 3 | Press secretary, editor of newsletter, projects director, field activities coordinator, deputy director of fund raising | 3-7 years |
| 4 | Press director, staff director, research methods specialist, director of governmental relations, general counsel | 7+ years |

## Job Responsibilities

### Entry Level

**THE BASICS:**   Answering phones. Filing and indexing on the computer. Photocopying, letter stuffing, acting as go-fer.

**MORE CHALLENGING DUTIES:**   Carrying out research, becoming involved with direct mail campaigns and membership drives, mapping voting patterns.

### Moving Up

The key to becoming a successful lobbyist is your ability to get the bills your interest group (or party) wants passed in the legislature. This takes a thorough knowledge of how the political system operates at the national, state, or local levels. It means getting to know key figures in both the political and private sectors who can directly affect the policies your group supports. It involves working closely with elected officials on developing legislation, working out wording, and devising amendments. The expertise this requires usually means higher education after a few years in the field: a law degree or fulfilling a masters degree in the subject area in which your interest group functions.

During the first few years that you work for a lobby or political party, you will go along on the rounds of hobnobbing with congressional aides, committee aides, and other interest group activists. You will witness, and then learn, the art of negotiating and forming coalitions.

## ADDITIONAL INFORMATION

### Salaries

Entry-level salaries in politics range from $12,000 to $14,000 per year. In mid-level jobs, such as a legislative aide, yearly salaries range from $30,000 to $40,000. Managers of national campaigns can earn as much as $50,000 per year.

## Working Conditions

*Hours:* Working hours within a campaign are long and often erratic. Twelve-hour days are not uncommon. Weekends and evenings are frequently times of particularly heavy work.

It is a rare political staffer who works a 9-to-5 day. Most congressional staff will regularly work an evening or two a week. When Congress is in session, the days are all long, and Saturdays and sometimes even Sundays become regular working days. Summer hours, except perhaps during campaign years, compensate by being much shorter.

Lobby and party work hours follow both congressional and campaign time schedules. Meetings with staffers, campaign workers, or members of other interest groups often take place over breakfast or on weekends.

*Environment:* Campaign headquarters are extremely noisy and full of activity. No matter how much space is available, it is never enough. Count on sharing space, probably even a telephone and typewriter (or computer) with someone else. If the campaign is successful, the noise level and the frenzy at headquarters will continue to rise until Election Day.

Congressional offices, both in Washington, DC, and in the state capitals, are busy and noisy. Staff usually occupies cramped quarters. Phones ring constantly, there are frequent visitors, and there is often a great deal of movement by staff from one room to another. Politics is a people business and thrives on a great deal of interaction.

Special interest group and party offices are similarly hectic. They are often more cramped (three to five people share a room) because of a lack of funds.

*Workstyle:* Campaigners, depending on the team you work with, can spend most of their day out on the road canvassing, setting up programs, etc. Others remain at their desks, answering the phones and handling all incoming problems as part of the support staff.

As a congressional or special interest group staffer, you spend much of your day at your desk or in office meetings. Research will take you out to various libraries, and you will occasionally attend committee hearings. Once you have reached the level of press secretary or LA, you spend much more of your time meeting with lobbyists, party supporters and other LAs.

*Travel:*    Campaigning, especially on an advance team, involves quite a bit of travel all over the district, state, or country. The amount varies widely, but it can reach the point where you are on the road almost constantly. Congressional staff members in Washington, DC, occasionally travel with their congressional representative, especially if they come from the same state or home district. House members are allowed 26 free round trips home each year, while senators are allotted 40. Occasionally, a representative will travel to a foreign country as a member of a fact-finding or other type of mission, and will take a select number of personal staff members along.

Public interest group staffers, especially those whose organizations operate on a national level, may travel to meet with their counterparts in other locations, or to attend conferences or conventions.

## Extracurricular Activities/Work Experience

Local or national campaigns—canvassing, polling, stuffing envelopes, etc.

Campus political organizations—fund raising, writing, organizing meetings and parties

Student government—on-campus campaigning, organizing large-scale activities, negotiating

Campus publications or stringer for local paper—writing, reporting selling ad space

Community service projects—aiding permanent staff in team work, writing, initiating new projects

## Internships

Each summer, hundreds of legislators, partisan and nonpartisan interest groups, the chief executive, and many government agencies and offices sponsor internship programs. Some are paid; most are not. Many internships are open to college juniors and seniors. A few are geared to graduate students with more specific training.

Most colleges and universities have internship placement offices which have access to information about specific internships. There are also a number of internship clearinghouses that match applicants with openings in a wide range of agencies.

Listings of internship program sponsors in Washington, DC, and throughout the nation are also easily available and updated each year. Besides the directories mentioned at the start of this volume (see "What's in This Book for You?") there are the following resources:

> City Volunteer Corps, Office of the Mayor
> 200 North Spring Street, Room 2200
> Los Angeles, CA 90012
> (The City Volunteer Corps places 200 interns in city
>      government each year.)

> *Guide to Government and Public Service*
> Office of Career Services and Off-Campus Learning
> Harvard University
> 54 Dunster Street
> Cambridge, MA 02138

> *Internbook* (published 3 times a year)
> Rhode Island Intern/Volunteer Consortium
> 274 Weybossett Street
> Providence, RI 02903
> (They place 300 interns in state and city government.)

> *Jobs in Social Change*
> Social and Educational Research Foundation
> 3416 Sansom St.
> Philadelphia, PA 19104

## Recommended Reading

**BOOKS**

*Both Ends of the Avenue: The Presidency, the Executive Branch, and Congress in the 1980s,* Anthony King, ed., American Enterprise Institute for Public Policy Research: 1983

*How to Win an Election: A Complete Guide to Running a Successful Campaign* by Sandy Huseby, St. Martin's Press: 1983

*How to Win Votes in the Politics of 1980* by Edward N. Costikyan, Harcourt Brace Jovanovich: 1980

*Parties, Elections and Representation in the State of New York* by Howard A. Scarrow, New York University Press: 1983

*Women and Politics: The Visible Majority* by Sandra Baxter and Majorie Lansing, University of Michigan: 1983

**PERIODICALS**

*Congress Quarterly* (quarterly), 1414 Twenty-second Street, N.W., Washington, DC 20037

*Foreign Affairs* (quarterly), Council on Foreign Relations, Inc., 58 East 68th Street, New York, NY 10021

*Public Opinion* (quarterly), Columbia University, 116th Street and Broadway, New York, NY 10027

## Professional Associations

Academy of Political Science
2852 Broadway
New York, NY 10025

American Academy of Political and Social Science
3937 Chestnut Street
Philadelphia, PA 19104

American Enterprise Institute for Public Policy Research
1150 Seventh Street, N.W.
Washington, DC 20036

American Political Science Association
1527 New Hampshire Avenue, N.W.
Washington, DC 20036

Public Interest Research Group
1346 Connecticut Avenue, Room 413
Washington, DC 20036

# INTERVIEWS

**Susan Hattan, Age 32**
**Legislative Director**
**Office of U.S. Senator Nancy Kassebaum, Washington, DC**

One summer during my college years, I worked in Washington, DC, as an intern for the representative from my district. I developed a great liking for the city and upon graduation (with a degree in political science and Spanish) I landed a job with Senator Robert Dole of my home state of Kansas.

The first position I held was that of staff assistant, helping to manage Senator Dole's mailing list. After working with the computerized mail and mailing lists, I was given the additional responsibility of answering correspondence. Next I moved from the annex with all of the machines to the main office to do correspondence work 100 percent of the time. Then, in addition to doing communications work, I was put in charge of correspondence for the entire office, determining who worked on which issues. From the overall picture of what the mail was saying I was able to keep the administrative assistant informed. From that position on I moved on to assisting with different legislative projects on an assigned basis.

During three of the four years I worked for Senator Dole, I attended graduate school at night, studying for an M.A. in American politics. It was difficult to go to school at night while working, especially in 1976 when Senator Dole ran for the vice presidency with President Gerald Ford .

My next job was with the Department of Agriculture. I was there only a year. I spent most of my time writing on many issues, so I got a good sense of what was going on in the agency.

In January 1979 I joined Senator Nancy Kassebaum's staff. It is critically important for senators to have people on their staffs from their own states. Being a Kansan, knowing Kansas, and knowing how things worked on the Hill made me an attractive candidate for the position. If you are looking for your first job, it would be wise to start by contacting members from your own state's delegation. In this way, the one advantage you have over every other person just like you looking for a job is that you know the member's state or district.

I am now the senator's legislative director (LD). The office is not highly structured; therefore, in addition to being the LD I perform functions of a legislative assistant. My main function as LD is to coordinate the office activity and to ensure that two people are not doing the same thing and that at least one person is doing everything that needs to be done. My responsibilities include giving advice and being available for people to come to and ask, "Who does this?"

I like the variety of my job. I enjoy having a number of issues to look at each day. There is no stagnation, and the activity is intoxicating sometimes. The most difficult adjustment to make is dealing with erratic and long hours. Another problem is having to deal with a lot of inflated, easily bruised egos.

My advice to college students interested in pursuing a career in politics is to become involved in local party politics, because that is where you are most likely to find out if you enjoy the environment, and where you are most likely to make contacts.

**Neel Lattimore, Age 23**
**Assistant to the Media Coordinator for the National Democratic Convention**
**Democratic National Committee, Washington, DC**

In college I was really involved in school government. I never got involved in anything political, although campus groups like the Young Democrats did exist. I was in charge of orientation, putting together programs for incoming students. I wrote booklets and other materials, following them through from idea to finished product.

My major was radio,television, and motion picture, with an emphasis on journalism. When I graduated, I wanted to get involved in a broad spectrum of media and work with people. Although I did not have an internship in politics, I think my background, all the writing I did for orientation, really helped me get my job. Competition is pretty tough. You have to be very persistent and keep in contact with everyone you meet and interview with.

I started off as assistant to the press secretary. Mass mailings are an important aspect to any kind of work in the press department. I also work a lot with the computer, filing and logging things into it such as credentials for the press. It's pretty tedious work but it has to be done. I answer a lot of questions on the phone, I do some research, and I do a lot of footwork: photocopying and sometimes driving a visiting press secretary around town.

One of the most disappointing things about the job is that I do so little writing. In fact, many of the skills you build in college you find you don't use in your first job. You're at the bottom of the pole—you have to start from scratch. It can be very frustrating. I will look at a press release one of the press secretaries has written and I think, "I can do that." But in fact, I probably can't. Writing a press release requires a style that is short and concise and gets the point across in as few words as possible. I need more experience before I will feel that I can write a good press release.

I love the excitement and pace of the job. The atmosphere is friendly and yet really high key. One of the best things about working in politics is that you work for a specific end product. You can see what you're working toward. Who knows? Someday you might even be working for the future President of the United States.

# BIBLIOGRAPHY

*The College Graduate's Career Guide* by Robert Ginn, Jr., Charles Scribner's Sons: 1981

*College Placement Annual* by the College Placement Council: revised annually (available in most campus placement offices)

*The Complete Job-Search Handbook: All the Skills You Need to Get Any Job and Have a Good Time Doing It* by Howard Figler, Holt, Rinehart & Winston: 1981

*Consider Your Option: Business Opportunities for Liberal Arts Graduates* by Christine A. Gould, Association of American Colleges: 1983 (free)

*Go Hire Yourself an Employer* by Richard K. Irish, Doubleday & Company: 1977

*The Hidden Job Market for the 80's* by Tom Jackson and Davidyne Mayleas, Times Books: 1981

*Jobs for English Majors and Other Smart People* by John L. Munschauer, Peterson's Guides: 1982

*Job Hunting with Employment Agencies* by Eve Gowdey, Barron's Educational Series: 1978

*Making It Big in the City* by Peggy J. Schmidt, Coward-McCann: 1983

*Making It on Your First Job* by Peggy J. Schmidt, Avon Books: 1981

*National Directory of Addresses and Telephone Numbers*, Concord Reference Books: revised annually

*The National Job-Finding Guide* by Heinz Uhrich and J. Robert Connor, Doubleday & Company: 1981

*The Perfect Résumé* by Tom Jackson, Doubleday & Company: 1981

*Put Your Degree to Work: A Career Planning and Job Hunting Guide for the New Professional* by Marcia R. Fox, W.W. Norton: 1979

*The Student Entrepreneur's Guide* by Brett M. Kingston, Ten Speed Press: 1980

*What Color Is Your Parachute? A Practical Manual for Job Hunters and Career Changers* by Richard N. Bolles, Ten Speed Press: 1983

*Where Are the Jobs?* by John D. Erdlen and Donald H. Sweet, Harcourt Brace Jovanovich: 1982

# INDEX

# NOTES

# NOTES